INSURANCE
MANUAL
FOR LIBRARIES

INSURANCE MANUAL FOR LIBRARIES

GERALD E. MYERS, CPCU, CLU

AMERICAN LIBRARY ASSOCIATION

Chicago 1977

Library of Congress Cataloging in Publication Data

Myers, Gerald E.
    Insurance manual for libraries.

    Includes index.
    1. Libraries—Insurance—Handbooks, manuals, etc.
I. American Library Association. II. Title.
Z683.5.M94   368.1   77-24524
ISBN 0-8389-0236-7

Copyright © 1977 by the American Library Association

    All rights reserved. No part of this publication
    may be reproduced in any form without permission
    in writing from the publisher, except by a reviewer
    who may quote brief passages in a review.

Printed in the United States of America

CONTENTS

PREFACE   xi

INTRODUCTION   xiii
    Objectives / xiii

1.   **A PHILOSOPHY OF INSURANCE FOR LIBRARIES**   1
- A.   Responsibility of the Library Board of Directors / 1
- B.   The Librarian's Responsibility / 2
- C.   The Risk Management Concept / 2
- D.   A Risk Management Policy Statement / 3

2.   **PROCEDURES FOR HANDLING THE INSURANCE PROGRAM**   5
- A.   Professional Assistance / 5
- B.   The Insurance Consultant / 6
- C.   Choosing an Insurance Agent or Broker / 7
- D.   Services Expected of the Agent / 8
- E.   Cooperation by the Library / 8
- F.   Services Available from Insurance Companies / 8
- G.   Types of Insurers / 9
- H.   Procedure for Regular Review of the Insurance Program / 9

3.   **ANALYSIS OF RISKS**   10
- A.   Kinds of Property / 10
  - 1. Buildings / 10

    2. Improvements and betterments / 10
    3. Furniture and fixtures and equipment / 10
    4. Books and library materials / 11
    5. Fine arts, rare books, original paintings / 11
    6. Consumable supplies and materials / 11
    7. Valuable records / 11
    8. Electronic data / 11
    9. Property of employees / 12
   10. Property of others / 12

B. Perils / 13
    1. Fire and lightning / 13
    2. Extended coverage / 13
       a. Windstorm, cyclone, tornado, and hail / 13
       b. Explosion (except steam boiler) / 13
       c. Aircraft and vehicle damage / 13
       d. Smoke damage (from faulty heating plants) / 13
       e. Riot, including riot attending a strike and civil commotion / 13
    3. Vandalism and malicious mischief / 13
    4. Sonic boom / 13
    5. Sprinkler leakage / 13
    6. Water damage from defective plumbing, heating, and air conditioning systems / 13
    7. Collapse of buildings or structures / 13
    8. Glass breakage (from other than designated perils) / 13
    9. Burglary, theft, robbery / 13
   10. Employee dishonesty / 13
   11. Steam boiler explosion / 13
   12. Transit / 13
   13. Earthquake / 13
   14. Flood, backing up of sewers, surface waters / 13

C. Liability for Torts / 14
    1. Bodily injury / 14
    2. Personal injury / 14
    3. Civil and constitutional rights violations / 14
    4. Property damage / 14

CONTENTS   vii

- D. Sources of Liability / 15
    1. Premises / 15
    2. Operations / 15
    3. Contracts / 15
    4. Autos, trucks, mobile equipment / 15
    5. Directors' (or trustees') and officers' liability / 15
    6. Civil and constitutional rights / 15
- E. Miscellaneous Insurable Risks / 16
    1. Injury to employees / 16
    2. Employee dishonesty / 16
    3. Steam boiler / 16
    4. Plate glass / 16
    5. Property in transit / 17
    6. Extra expense / 17

4. APPRAISALS AND VALUATION OF PROPERTY   18

- A. In General / 18
- B. Buildings / 18
- C. Improvements and Betterments in Leased Buildings / 19
- D. Furniture and Fixtures and Equipment / 20
- E. Books and Library Materials / 21
    1. Source of values / 21
    2. Adjustment of *Bowker Annual* figures / 21
    3. Summary of procedures to be used in pricing / 22
- F. Other Tangible Property / 22

5. INSURANCE COVERAGES, POLICIES, AND POLICY FORMS   24

- A. In General / 24
- B. Blanket Property—Buildings and Contents / 24
- C. The Public and Institutional Property (P.I.P.) Form / 25
- D. Special Property Endorsements / 26
    1. Contingent liability / 26
    2. Large deductibles / 26

3. Replacement cost / 26
4. Special pricing / 27
E. Books and Library Materials / 28
1. Blanket Contents form / 28
2. Valuable Papers form / 28
3. Special library policy / 29
4. Recommendation / 29
F. Large Deductible (Self-Retention) Plans / 30
G. Miscellaneous Property Coverages / 31
1. Fine arts / 31
2. Valuable records / 31
3. Bailee liability / 31
4. Transportation floater / 32
5. Plate glass / 32
6. Steam boiler explosion / 32
7. Burglary and theft of personal property / 33
8. Money and securities / 33
9. Flood insurance / 33
10. Difference in (of) conditions (D.I.C. or D.O.C.) / 33
H. Comprehensive Public Liability / 34
1. Limits of liability / 34
2. Employees as additional insureds / 34
3. Personal injury / 34
4. Contractual liability / 35
5. Products liability / 35
6. Dram shop liability / 35
7. Property of others / 35
I. Auto Liability / 35
1. Owned vehicles / 35
2. Physical damage / 36
3. Non-owned auto liability / 36
J. Umbrella (Excess) Liability / 36
K. Employee Dishonesty Bond / 37
L. Extra Expense for Resumption of Operations / 37
M. Workers' Compensation / 38

CONTENTS ix

- N. Directors', Officers', Trustees' Liability / 38
    1. Directors', Officers', and Trustees' form / 38
    2. Public Officials' Liability policy / 39
    3. Board of Education Liability or Public School Trustees' Liability / 39

6. NEW CONSTRUCTION 40

- A. In General / 40
- B. Insurance Review of Architect's Plans / 40
- C. The Hold Harmless Clause / 40
- D. Insurance Requirements for the Contractor / 41
- E. Owners' Protective Liability Insurance / 41
- F. Surety (Performance) Bond / 41
- G. Builders' Risk Insurance / 42

7. INSURANCE RATES AND PREMIUMS 43

- A. Property (Fire) Insurance Rates / 43
- B. Workers' Compensation Rates / 43
- C. Other Insurance Classes / 44

8. LOSS PREVENTION, PROTECTION, AND SAFETY 45

- A. In General / 45
- B. Insurance Company Inspections / 45
- C. Local Fire Department Inspections / 45
- D. Fire Protection Standards / 45
- E. Outside Protection and Security / 46
- F. Fire and Burglar Alarms / 46
- G. Automatic Sprinklers / 47
- H. Halon® an Extinguishing Agent / 47
- I. Protection from Pilferage / 47
- J. Microfilming the Shelflist / 48
- K. Duplicating Magnetic Tapes and Discs / 48
- L. OSHA Requirements / 48

x   *Contents*

9.   **LOSSES AND CLAIMS**   49
  A. In General   /   49
  B. Prompt Reporting of Losses and Accidents   /   49
  C. Proof of Loss   /   50
  D. Cooperation with the Liability Insurance Company   /   50
  E. Salvage Operations   /   50

APPENDIXES   51
  A. Sample Risk Management Policy Statement for the Small or Medium-Sized Public Library   /   51
  B. Sample Risk Management Policy Statement for the Large Public Library or Institutional Library   /   53
  C. Example of Valuation Study (New Library Facility)   /   54
  D. Analysis of Insurable Values   /   56
  E. Special Library Policy—Report of Values   /   58
  F. A Typical Analysis of *Bowker Annual* Prices   /   59
  G. Checklist for Library Insurance   /   60

GLOSSARY   61

PREFACE

This manual was initiated by the Insurance for Libraries Committee (chaired at the time by Donald L. Ungarelli) of the Library Organization Management Section (LOMS), Library Administration Division, American Library Association. It represents an updating and expansion of an earlier manual prepared under the auspices of the Bur Oak, DuPage, Northern Illinois, North Suburban, Starved Rock, and Suburban Library Systems of northern Illinois for use by their member libraries.

The concept of a practical "how-to-do-it" insurance manual was envisioned first by Joanne Klene, Chief Consultant for the Suburban Library System, Hinsdale, Illinois, in the early 1970s to provide answers to the questions about insurance and the administration of a library's insurance program which were plaguing its librarians. To supply a needed service to public libraries which his system and others serve, Lester L. Stoffel, Executive Director of the Suburban Library System, brought together five other library systems for the purpose of underwriting an insurance manual.

Acknowledgment is made to Phillip L. Maxfield, current Chairperson of the Insurance for Libraries Committee, and other members of the committee who have reviewed the manuscript and offered valuable suggestions, and to Herbert Bloom, Senior Editor, American Library Association, for his editorial expertise and guidance.

INTRODUCTION

The original manual on this subject by the author was limited in scope because the member libraries which it was designed to serve were a homogeneous group, their needs and problems fairly uniform. The present work has been expanded to apply to the vast and varied membership of the American Library Association. Recognition is given to the problems of the very small as well as the very large public library and to the special problems in valuations and insurance coverages for institutional and professional libraries and special collections.

OBJECTIVES

This manual utilizes the relatively new and professional "Risk Management" approach. Its specific objectives are:

1. To inform trustees, directors, and library personnel of the essential elements of an appropriate insurance program and of the risk management concepts to be used in establishing that program

2. To assist those responsible for administering and implementing a program, librarians as well as insurance agents and brokers.

3. To provide a guide and a checklist for the library so that the burden for proper insurance coverage can be placed to a considerable extent on the insurance agent or broker whom the library has engaged, and, in addition, the means by which the effectiveness of its insurance program can be judged.

Because this is an insurance manual, not an insurance text, it is expected that the librarian and the insurance agent will follow it in the sequence in which it is arranged. However, the reader may, on occasion, be particularly interested in a certain type of risk coverage or property coverage or a special insurance coverage.

It should be noted that within the risk management framework of this manual, any of the subjects may be treated in two or three separate chapters. These are chapter 3, "Analysis of Risk"; chapter 4, "Appraisals and Valuation of Property"; and chapter 5, "Insurance Coverages, Policies, and Policy Forms." For example, insurance for books and library materials are dealt with in Section A 4 of chapter 3, section E of chapter 4, and section E of chapter 5.

A careful review of the detailed table of contents should increase the value of this manual for the reader.

Discussion of group insurance for employees has been purposely omitted from this manual. The insurance needs of employees—hospital, medical, and disability insurance—are not unique to libraries.

1

A PHILOSOPHY OF INSURANCE FOR LIBRARIES

A. **RESPONSIBILITY OF THE LIBRARY BOARD OF DIRECTORS**

Whether the library is a part of an institution or other organization or is a separate legal entity, the ultimate authority for its operation will rest in a board of directors (or trustees). The obligations and responsibilities of this board may be defined by state statute, or the board may, to a large extent, be subject to common law rules. In any event, there will be a moral, if not a legal, obligation calling for the exercise of good business judgment in protecting the assets of the library against serious loss. This might justify "no insurance" for a remote hazard or for a small loss exposure. It will not justify the directors abandoning the obligation for the purchase of insurance to another public body, such as a municipality if the library is a part of that municipality, nor to the comptroller of the institution, nor even to the librarian, unless standards or guidelines delegating authority to purchase insurance have been established.

Discharge of the responsibility for maintaining proper insurance protection, like that of other business decisions, has become more significant in recent years, as evidenced by lawsuits against directors of business corporations who have been sued with increasing frequency because of dissatisfaction of stockholders where directors have failed to use good judgment in making business decisions affecting the corporation.

Even though the library is a nonprofit or quasi-governmental entity with no stockholders who might bring suit for loss because of poor judgment or negligent decisions on the part of directors, there are classes of people who may lose benefits which are of value to them. A curtailment of services or loss of facilities through negligent action of directors or trustees may be the basis for a class action by such beneficiaries. For example, the directors may cause a financial loss by failing to engage a competent contractor for a new building project, or by neglecting to require a financial audit, or by carelessly engaging incompetent or dishonest employees.

More recently lawsuits have been directed against public school board members for negligence in their duties or for improper business decisions. Although very few lawsuits have been directed against library trustees for failing to perform properly, the trend in other fields emphasizes the heavy responsibility which the law is placing upon directors and trustees generally.

B. THE LIBRARIAN'S RESPONSIBILITY

Normally the board will delegate responsibility for establishing and maintaining a proper insurance program to the librarian, either directly or through an Insurance Committee of the board. This delegation of responsibility should include certain guidelines, and, as in the case of other areas of business activity, it should also require periodic reports to the board.

Even where the responsibility for administering the library insurance program rests with an officer of an institution of which it is a part, certain responsibilities should be delegated by that individual to the librarian. The library and its insurance needs are unique. It has special valuation problems and the services for those it is designed to serve cannot be readily provided by the use of substitute facilities. In most cases it is only the librarian who can be relied upon for information essential to the establishment of an adequate insurance program.

Where the institution of which the library is a part has a professional risk manager or full-time insurance buyer, the librarian should insist upon an explanation of the coverages provided, the amount of deductible the library may be called upon to absorb, the extent of recovery which can be expected in event of loss in relation to cost of repairing the damage: in other words the strain, if any, which may be put on the library's budget by any probable loss.

Whether the library is a small public library or part of a very large institution, a policy statement is desirable as a guide for the librarian. This should embody the risk management concept which is discussed later and it should contain parameters relating to limits of liability, catastrophe risks to be provided for, and allowable limits of deductibles or self-insured losses. (*Refer to* Appendixes A and B).

C. THE RISK MANAGEMENT CONCEPT

Within the last decade or two, larger insurance buyers have come to view the purchase of insurance as part of a broader function known as "risk management." This concept recognizes that some risks can be reduced or eliminated; that some can be transferred to others; that some risks are insurable, some not; and that some risks involve types of losses which should be insured against and others are losses which can be assumed or self-insured. These principles are readily adaptable to libraries, large or small, public, private, or special and can be applied as follows:

1. Determine the risks of loss to which the library is subject.
2. Assume (that is, self-insure) those risks which
   a. Are so small in amount as to present no financial problem (e.g., loss of books in the possession of individual borrowers), or
   b. Are so remote that good business judgment justifies ignoring the risk (e.g., earthquake in certain areas of the country), or
   c. Occur with high frequency or with reasonable certainty so that the probable total annual loss can be predicted. In such cases, the premium for insurance will probably exceed the predictable losses (for example, loss of books due to theft or vandalism). In some instances, as in the case of auto collision insurance, the library can reduce its premium cost by assuming a reasonable deductible per loss.
3. Reduce the risk where possible (e.g., by reducing excessive cash accumulations with more frequent bank deposits or installing fire extinguishers or automatic sprinklers with resulting reduction in fire insurance rates); eliminate the risk (for example, by disposing of a truck used to transport books and hiring a public trucker for this purpose); or transfer the risk to others (e.g., by a "hold harmless" or indemnity clause in a construction contract whereby the contractor assumes all liability for accidents to workmen and others arising out of the new construction).
4. Insure all other risks which can be insured (that is, which are of an insurable nature). It is important to recognize that in certain areas insurance companies may have expertise and provide valuable services which justify the purchase of insurance even though the library has the financial capacity to absorb the losses which might be expected. (*Refer also* to chap. 3, E. 3.)

D.   A RISK MANAGEMENT POLICY STATEMENT

Within the concept of risk management, there should be a well-established policy statement from the governing body or chief executive of the library under which the risk management principles can be applied. This policy should take into consideration the financial condition of the library, its access to additional funds for uninsured losses, and its obligation to those whom it undertakes to serve as respects continuation of its present services.

The risk management policy statement of the library should designate the individual or individuals who shall have the administrative responsibility. It should serve as a guide to limits of liability and perils to be insured against and to the amount and extent of insurance policy deductibles which can be safely permitted. It may designate the types of services to be used, that is, consultants, agents, or brokers, and it may prescribe requirements relating to bidding of insurance coverages. (Typical risk management policy statements for both public and institutional libraries are contained in Appendixes A and B.)

2

PROCEDURES FOR HANDLING THE INSURANCE PROGRAM

A. PROFESSIONAL ASSISTANCE

The professional assistance which the librarian needs in handling the insurance program may come from one or more of the following three sources:

1. If the library is very large or is part of a very large institution, its insurance and risk management program may be placed in the hands of a professional, full-time risk manager.

2. An insurance consultant may be engaged on a continuing basis to act on behalf of the library in the capacity of professional risk manager or he/she may be engaged periodically to review insurance risks and coverages, prepare specifications for bidding, and assist in loss settlements.

3. The small or medium-sized library may find it more practical to choose an insurance agent or broker who will be charged with providing professional advice and service as well as placing the insurance.

   Generally, the agent or broker will be able to provide all of the neecssary services for the compensation he or she receives in the form of commission on the policies he or she issued. The consultant, on the other hand, will require a fee based on time spent on the account. The cost of consultation will be in addition to the commission paid to an agent or broker. This fee may be justified in some instances because the consultant will have an opportunity for wider choice of markets and therefore lower premium costs, or because agents or brokers may be willing to offer policies at lower commission rates where a consultant has been engaged to provide certain insurance services.

   The argument is made that only a consultant on a fee basis will possess the objectivity necessary for a professional job, that an agent or broker compensated by a percentage of commissions lacks the incentive to reduce premium costs which would lower his/her own commissions. This may be true in some cases, but there are means of measuring the effectiveness of an agent or broker just as there are of the consultant; besides, the intense competition in the insurance business usually mitigates against this possibility. On the other hand, a consultant may overstate his/her hours. In insurance, as in other areas of business and professional services, the quality of services the library receives will depend on the people it chooses to do business with.

If the library feels obliged to place insurance with more than one insurance agent or broker, to avoid gaps in coverage it should either engage a consultant to supervise the entire insurance program or arrange for one of its agents or brokers to accept the responsibility for the entire program. In some instances a fee in addition to the brokerage commission may be justified and allowed when the broker assumes obligations and service requirements in excess of those which might normally be contemplated by commissions on policies he/she writes.

B.   THE INSURANCE CONSULTANT

The primary need for an insurance consultant will occur when the library feels that it wishes an independent and objective survey of its risks and coverages or when it desires to secure bids for its various insurance coverages. Bidding is frequently by directive of the board of trustees, and in some cases it may be a statutory requirement for public bodies. In either event, the services of an insurance consultant are desirable for drafting specifications and making recommendations as to insurance markets from whom bids should be requested, much as an architect is necessary in preparing plans for a building and supervising bidding among contractors.

The preparation of the specifications will require first that the consultant be thoroughly familiar with the operations of the library and with the risks to which it is subject. He or she must be available to analyze bids when they are received to determine that they conform to the specifications and then to advise which should be accepted. The general practice is to request insurance bids no more often than triennially (unless unusual circumstances arise to require more frequent bidding); usually it will be difficult to persuade the better insurance markets to bid if coverages are not allowed to stay with the same market for at least three years.

C. **CHOOSING AN INSURANCE AGENT OR BROKER**

Generally, the insurance broker is considered to be an agent of the library, and the insurance agent an agent of the insurance company. However, the agent who is in the category of an "independent agent" representing many companies will act on behalf of the insured much as a broker. Only in certain limited instances such as binding coverage, collecting premium, and issuing policies or endorsements will he or she be an agent of the company and as a rule these activities will not interfere with his or her acting on behalf of the library.

A number of insurance companies operate with exclusive or "captive" agents, that is, agents who are not permitted to represent any other company. Such agents generally will not be able to operate in a legal relationship as agent of the library.

As it does when engaging professionals in other areas, the library should use appropriate criteria in selecting an insurance agent or broker, such as:

1. The reputation in the community of the individual (or firm)
2. His or her relationship with insurance companies
3. His or her experience in the field of public or institutional insurance
4. His or her general competence and professional training (of which the designation CPCU, Chartered Property Casualty Underwriter, will be positive evidence)
5. His or her willingness to provide the necessary insurance service on a continuing basis.

An insurance policy is of no real value until a loss occurs, at which point certain elements become critical. The insurance policies should be properly written, the name of insured correctly listed, the insurance company financially sound, properly licensed, and of good reputation. These criteria need not be of primary concern to the library if it has chosen a competent insurance agent.

The independent agent normally will have a number of companies from which he or she can secure premium quotations for library insurance. An agent may be in a position to draw up his or her own specifications and secure quotations from a number of these companies at regular intervals to furnish evidence to the library that he or she is providing insurance coverage at a reasonable cost.

As an additional safeguard, the library may occasionally invite an outside agent or company to review its insurance program both for coverages and cost. An agent generally will not object to this if he or she knows that the board desires and appreciates the service the agent is rendering and if he or she knows the board is not likely to replace him or her as agent for a modest cost reduction.

D. SERVICES EXPECTED OF THE AGENT

The agent should be expected to perform as a risk manager for the library. To accomplish this the agent must apply his or her expertise in risk management and insurance to the facts and circumstances relating to the property and operations of the library. Specifically the agent should be required to:

1. Analyze risks and review the insurance program periodically (at least annually).
2. Assist in developing values for insurance purposes.
3. Maintain insurance coverages in force in financially sound companies.
4. Assist in reporting claims and adjusting losses.
5. Be available for consultation on changes in operation and on new construction and their effect on the insurance program.

E. COOPERATION BY THE LIBRARY

No insurance agent can perform satisfactorily without full and complete cooperation of the insured. It is essential that some individual who is thoroughly familiar with the library's operations and plans be available for information and consultation. Usually this will be the librarian. The insurance program will be no better than the completeness and accuracy of the information supplied by the library. It is important also that there be an opportunity for securing decisions promptly on insurance matters.

F. SERVICES AVAILABLE FROM INSURANCE COMPANIES

Many insurance agencies and brokerage firms provide service facilities such as engineering and inspection services, appraisal service, and valuation counseling so that little in this area is required from the insurance companies. If these services are not available, then the insurance company or companies chosen should be able to provide such facilities. A regular inspection program should be established for safety and fire protection purposes. If a professional appraisal company has not been engaged for maintaining values, assistance in this area should be sought from the insurance company.

G. **TYPES OF INSURERS**

There are several classifications of insurance companies which may be of interest to librarians. The majority of those writing commercial, industrial, and institutional risks can provide most of the various types of insurance and the services referred to in the preceding paragraph F which the library will need.

These companies may be organized as stock or mutual insurance companies. Some of the latter may pay a dividend at the expiration of the policy for some types of insurance. Most of both stock and mutual companies operate through independent agents and brokers. A limited number operate only through exclusive or "captive" agents, that is, agents who represent only one company. Another small group is represented only by salespersons (employees).

Still another group of companies constitute the "excess" or "surplus line" market. Included in this group is Lloyd's of London. These companies will accept orders from agents and brokers and are most prominent in the areas of umbrella and excess liability and Directors and Officers liability insurance.

H. **PROCEDURE FOR REGULAR REVIEW OF THE INSURANCE PROGRAM**

The responsibility of the agent or broker for reviewing insurance regularly cannot be met unless he or she has the full cooperation of both the library staff and the board of directors. A regular review of the insurance program should be handled as a routine matter and the library board should include on its agenda at a regular meeting each year, an opportunity for a report on the insurance program. This report should be presented prior to policy expirations and the insurance agent should arrange to meet with the librarian beforehand so as to secure the necessary information.

3

ANALYSIS OF RISKS

This chapter contains a checklist of areas to consider for insurable hazards and risks of loss, and a brief explanation of the circumstances or events which are likely to cause loss.

A.   KINDS OF PROPERTY

The problem of appraisal and valuation of tangible property which is essential in order to properly insure the library against loss is discussed in chapter 4, "Appraisals and Valuation of Property." The following list is intended to include major items of property (1) which the library owns, uses, controls, or has responsibility for, and (2) whose loss or damage could result in financial loss.

1. *Buildings*

2. *Improvements and betterments.* This pertains to improvements in a leased building, such as permanent fixtures, new plumbing facilities, and the like, which have been made by the library as tenant under a current lease. In every case the lease should be reviewed to determine whether the landlord has an obligation to replace the improvements and betterments in the event of loss or damage. If the landlord does not have this legal obligation, then the library has two risks of loss:
    a. The cost of replacing the improvements, if they are damaged or destroyed, in order to continue to use the building
    b. The unamortized portion of the improvements and betterments or their "use" value for the unexpired terms of the lease, should the landlord cancel the lease as a result of the loss or damage.
    [The standard fire policy forms discussed in chapter 5, "Insurance Coverages, Policies, and Policy Forms," can be endorsed to insure both risks.]

3. *Furniture and fixtures and equipment.* Included in this category of

property are all forms of tangible personal property used in the operation of the library except books and library materials and licensed vehicles.

4. *Books and library materials.* The latter term is intended to include films, prints, tapes, recordings and all other materials which are intended for the use of patrons of the library.

5. *Fine arts, rare books, original paintings.* Such property should always be insured for a specific or stated value for each item (or group of similar items). The value may be the purchase price or an appraised value set by an expert in the field.

6. *Consumable supplies and materials.* Property in this category includes such items as office stationery, envelopes, library supplies, janitor supplies, and the like.

7. *Valuable records.* These are intangibles and include those records which have a value in excess of the actual tangible value of the cost of paper plus the cost of transcribing. Books are frequently insured under a valuable papers or valuable records policy although they are not strictly in the valuable records category since they are marketable items with a specific market or purchase price. Similarly, catalog cards are not, in the strict sense of the word, valuable papers because their value is measurable as the cost of the card plus the cost of labor in transcribing.

Where research or extra expense is necessary to accumulate information on the records, an intangible value may exist. For example, shelflist cards where no duplicate such as microfilm is available from which card information can be copied will require special expense in reconstruction. Special indexes of a local newspaper where a duplicate is not available and where research will be necessary to replace the index may involve an intangible value.

Many other library records, such as financial and accounting records, may have an intangible value and be extremely costly to duplicate, but they need not be insured if no attempt would be made to duplicate them.

8. *Electronic data.* With increasing frequency, library records and indexes are being maintained on magnetic tapes and discs. Insurance policies normally limit recovery to the cost of the tapes or discs in their unexposed or blank form. If duplicates are available,

the additional tangible value of the tape or disc can be expressed as the value of machine time in duplicating.

Because of the vast amount of information which can be stored on magnetic media, the only practical solution to risk of loss is to maintain duplicates at a detached, safe location.

9. *Property of employees.* Most property insurance forms covering the library will include coverage for property of employees, subject to a limit of say $100 to $500. Coverage will not be necessary for employees who carry a homeowners or tenants policy, provided the employee property is not "business property" and therefore excluded under the personal policy. If it is intended that employee "business property" or other personal property be included, consideration should be given to the deductible amount in the library policy and who shall suffer the deductible.

10. *Property of others* for which the library is responsible. This may include a large variety of property such as books, office machines, microfilming equipment, photostatic equipment, and so forth. The values may not be readily determinable nor the extent of responsibility of the library fixed. For example, if the library has made no promise to be responsible for loss or damage to the property, then its only liability will be that of a bailee which liability results from its failure to use "due care" in preserving the property. In such a situation the owner may have a risk of loss in some circumstances, and the library who holds the property, in others. The most economical method of insuring is to cover both interests in a single policy, although this may not be practical.

   a. If the library has a heavy moral obligation to the owner, it may wish to insure not only its own bailee (*see* Glossary) risk but also the interest of the owner, treating the property as its own.
   b. On the other hand, the library may have no desire to protect the owner and therefore it will insure only its "bailee liability."

   In the first instance, the value should be included with its own property. In the second, if value is substantial, it will be less costly to separately insure the bailee risk.

   Whether the library insures such property in the same policy as its own property or in a separate policy, an effort should be made to secure a commitment from the owner in writing as to the total value of the property so that the library knows the dollar limit of its liability.

ANALYSIS OF RISKS   13

B.   PERILS

The following is a list of common perils to which the library property may be subject. These may be referred to in insurance policies as insured perils. Some may appear as exclusions in an "all risk" policy. For an explanation and definition of each term, the specific policy should be referred to.

1. Fire and lightning
2. Extended coverage
   a. Windstorm, cyclone, tornado, and hail
   b. Explosion (except steam boiler)
   c. Aircraft and vehicle damage
   d. Smoke damage (from faulty heating plants)
   e. Riot, including riot attending a strike and civil commotion
3. Vandalism and malicious mischief
4. Sonic boom
5. Sprinkler leakage
6. Water damage from defective plumbing, heating, and air conditioning systems
7. Collapse of buildings or structures
8. Glass breakage (from other than designated perils)
9. Burglary, theft, robbery
10. Employee dishonesty
11. Steam boiler explosion
12. Transit including collision or upset (for example, of a transporting vehicle)
13. Earthquake
14. Flood, backing up of sewers, surface waters.

A broad form of coverage on property which may include many of the above perils is known as "all risks" coverage. This will specifically exclude certain uninsurable perils such as wear and tear, mechanical breakdown, erasure of magnetic recordings due to electrical or magnetic disturbance or errors in processing, inherent vice, loss through dishonesty of persons to whom the property is entrusted, and certain catastrophes among which are flood, earthquake, war, nuclear damage.

C.   LIABILITY FOR TORTS

Liability insurance is intended to protect the insured against claims for injuries to persons or property arising out of his/her torts, that is, his/her wrongful act or omission. Generally it applies to the so-called unintentional tort of negligence, although coverage is also available where the act is intentional but the injury unintended.

1. *Bodily injury.* This coverage is intended to apply to injuries to third persons (other than employees, whose injuries fall within a Workmen's Compensation Act) arising as a result of negligence of the library employees or agents. The term bodily injury includes death.

2. *Personal injury.* A broader term than "bodily injury," this includes certain additional torts which are listed in the standard liability forms as follows:

   "A. False Arrest, Detention or Imprisonment, or Malicious Prosecution

   "B. Libel, Slander, Defamation or Violation of Right of Privacy

   "C. Wrongful Entry or Eviction or Other Invasion of Right of Privacy."

   (The standard "personal injury" endorsement excludes coverage for claims made against the library by employees. For a modest premium this exclusion can usually be eliminated.)

3. *Civil and constitutional rights violations.* These may now be the basis of law suits under a federal statute (*see* para. D.6, following). Insurance coverage is not generally available, unless under a separate and somewhat limited policy.

4. *Property damage.* Refers to the liability of the library for damage to property of others. This is especially important where the library building is located in a congested area and where a negligent fire or explosion might damage neighboring property. The standard liability policy does not cover liability for damage to property in the care, custody or control of, or used or occupied by the insured.

D. SOURCES OF LIABILITY

Liability may arise from negligent actions of employees or agents or failure in a duty owed to the public resulting in damage or injury. The most common circumstances involve:

1. *Premises.* Building(s), grounds, leased property
2. *Operations* or activities, including those of employees, agents, and board members
3. *Contracts* in which the library has agreed to indemnify or hold harmless the other party for liability for injuries arising out of the contract. (In the case of new construction, the library will be the beneficiary of such a clause wherein the contractor agrees to hold harmless the library.) Indemnity agreements in leases, sidewalk permits, easements, elevator maintenance agreements will be automatically insured under a standard liability policy. Others should be carefully analyzed and insured by special endorsement.
4. *Autos,* trucks, mobile equipment, whether owned by or leased or hired by the library, as well as vehicles owned by others which are being driven on library business
5. *Directors' (or trustees') and officers' liability* is a general area of liability risk to which directors or trustees and officers may be subject and which is not covered by the standard liability insurance policy. This constitutes more of a threat than a reality at this time for public and nonprofit corporations and is a risk similar to that intended to be covered by the directors and officers (D&O) policy written for business corporations. This type of policy undertakes to protect the directors and officers who might be sued by a shareholder on behalf of the corporation in a derivative action where the directors or officers have acted negligently or with poor business judgment and caused financial loss to the corporation.

    In the case of a nonprofit corporation or a public (that is, governmental or quasi-governmental) body a similar action might be brought by a member or by a citizen whom the corporation or public body is organized to serve.

6. *Civil and constitutional rights* involve another area of risk to which directors, trustees, and officers may be subject but which may also involve other individuals and organizations. The liability has been created by a federal statute entitled "Civil action for deprivation of rights," Title 42, sec. 1983. This statute affords a basis for suit by

an individual whose civil or constitutional rights have been violated. (In a recent New Jersey case a Superior Court judge awarded a judgment to a teacher of a community college for violation of the teacher's rights in connection with her discharge. Judgment was awarded in the amount of $10,000 against each of six college trustees, individually.) Schools and library boards may have to face suits by women who claim they have been deprived of advancement solely on the basis of their sex.

E.   MISCELLANEOUS INSURABLE RISKS

1. *Injury to employees.* Public bodies including libraries usually are subject to the Workmen's Compensation Act and should be covered by workers' compensation insurance. The individual state law should be consulted in this regard. In any event, the insurance is desirable because it provides indemnity for the injured employee and protection for the library. The standard policy will include an employer's liability limit of $100,000 for claim for employee injury which does not come within the Act.

2. *Employee dishonesty.* This is normally insured under a fidelity bond. It is a risk not limited to the treasurer of the library or those in a supervisory capacity since the risk involves loss of property as well as money. Coverage should be on a blanket basis so that all employees are covered without being specifically named.

3. *Steam boiler.* In the occasional instance where buildings are heated by steam, a special steam boiler explosion policy is required because the fire and extended coverage policy does not include steam boiler explosion. The insurance company always provides professional inspection services. The inspector is licensed by the state (or municipality) and his inspection satisfies the inspection requirements of the state or municipal code. In some instances it may be desirable to insure hot water boilers (even though a hot water boiler explosion is not excluded under the fire and extended coverage policy) so that the insurance company inspection can be used to satisfy the governmental inspection requirements for this type of heating plant.

4. *Plate glass.* The most common breaks result from vandalism, accidental, or unknown causes. The usual building fire and extended coverage policy covers glass breakage from the named perils but excludes glass breakage by vandals. If unusually large and costly plates are subject to such breakage, separate "plate glass" insurance

may be desirable. It may also be desirable to insure if there are a very large number of plates subject to breakage at one time. Generally, self-insurance is justified because individual losses are not large. If, however, there is a high frequency of such losses, insurance may be very costly or may not be obtainable.

5. *Property in transit.* Where library property is away from the premises, as in mobile units or temporarily on loan in substantial amounts subject to a single loss, it may be desirable to insure under a transportation floater policy. This will require an estimate of total values at risk and a list of locations where the property is usually kept. Coverage will apply while temporarily at location and while in transit.

Whether the property out on loan to libraries from a system or from other libraries should be insured by the owner will depend on the contractual relations with the bailee, that is, on whether the bailee has assumed all risk of loss or damage to the property while it is on bailee's premises.

6. *Extra expense.* An indirect loss can result from serious damage to library property in the form of extra or additional expense if the library desires to continue its services at temporary locations. Since the library's major income does not depend upon continued service but is derived from tax income or a budget figure from its parent institution or organization, the extra expense may not be necessary as it would be for a business enterprise, such as a bank. The library should determine in advance whether it will need an extra fund of money to continue facilities at temporary locations in the event of a serious catastrophe. If so, it should then determine the amount of extra or unusual expenses which might be necessary to continue operation and for what period of time. This will be the basis of extra expense insurance.

Extra expense insurance may be desirable also for larger libraries or systems that have installed extensive electronic data processing (EDP) equipment. The measure of loss and amount of coverage needed will depend upon rental charges for similar equipment elsewhere and the estimated time to repair or replace the insured's damaged equipment. Of critical importance is the availability of substitute equipment in the event of insured loss or uninsured breakdown of the library's or system's installations. At least tentative plans should be made for use of outside equipment in the event of emergency.

4

APPRAISALS AND VALUATION OF PROPERTY

A. IN GENERAL

Except in the case of fine arts or valuable papers where the insurance company will agree on a value for loss settlement in advance, property losses may be adjusted on one of two bases: (1) replacement cost if replaced, that is, the actual cost of replacement without deduction for depreciation; (2) actual cash value, defined as the market value of a "marketable" item (such as a used typewriter, used furniture, etc.), or replacement cost less depreciation for buildings and for personal property not available on the "used" market. The depreciation factor is not easily determined, but there are certain standards or guides which can be relied upon. Consideration is given to age, condition, extent of usage, obsolescence, utility value, and the like.

Where the property insured is not available at a depreciated price (as are used typewriters, adding machines, etc.), or where the library would prefer to replace the damaged or lost property with new property instead of used, consideration should be given to insuring on replacement cost basis. This requires a higher amount of insurance and a larger premium, but it protects the library reserves and it may avoid a referendum to raise additional funds to make up the difference between the insurance recovery on an actual cash value basis and the replacement cost. Replacement cost coverage is especially important for buildings because they can be repaired or replaced only at the full cost of new materials and labor.

The key to a proper insurance program for protection of property is the appraisal or valuation. If a reliable value is established initially, this can be trended from year to year by the use of cost tables or indexes available from many sources which are available to insurance companies and insurance agents and brokers.

B. BUILDINGS

The source of initial valuation for buildings, not necessarily listed in order of cost or expense to the library nor reliability, are:

1. Original construction costs, excluding land values, landscaping, the cost of underground foundations, and other noninsurable values, adjusted for increases in construction costs from the date of construction to the present time. This method will be reliable only if the original cost was a reasonable one, that is, if the contractor who built the building realized a fair but not excessive profit, or if the original bids for the construction fell within a fairly narrow range.
2. Estimate of present day replacement cost by the library's architect, especially if he designed the building originally or is familiar with it by virtue of additions or remodeling.
3. An insurance appraisal by the library's insurance agent or insurance company, if either is equipped and willing to furnish this service.
4. A professional appraisal by an appraisal company specializing in insurance appraisals. This procedure will be most costly but will probably contain considerable construction and cost detail which will be of help in proving and adjusting a serious loss.

The depreciation factor may vary from ⅜ percent to ½ percent per year of age for superior construction with excellent maintenance, to 1 percent or more per year for inferior buildings with poor to fair maintenance. Seldom will the total depreciation exceed 35 percent to 40 percent for an old building if well maintained unless there is substantial obsolescence.

Because the building rate is generally lower than the contents rate, attention should be given to the policy definition of "building." This includes "fixtures, machinery and equipment constituting a part of and pertaining to the service of the building" and, in general, applies to permanent shelving; counters; stacks; heating, air conditioning and plumbing equipment; and permanent electrical installations for building service. Intercom installations may be part of building values; telephone and radio equipment generally will not be, nor will EDP installations.

C. IMPROVEMENTS AND BETTERMENTS IN LEASED BUILDINGS

The valuation should be determined in the same manner as for buildings but with no depreciation if replacement is the obligation of the tenant (i.e., the library). If the landlord has the obligation of replacement but also has the option of cancellation of the lease in the event of fire loss, then the measure of recovery for the library will usually be the unamortized leasehold value, that is, that proportion of the original cost to the library for the improvements as represented by the unexpired portion of the lease.

D.   FURNITURE AND FIXTURES AND EQUIPMENT

A detailed inventory is essential both for arriving at a total insurable value and for establishing or proving a loss. The greater the detail in description of each item, the more readily can value be established for the adjuster. However, it should not be necessary to list minor items. These frequently can be "lumped" together when the total amount is not large. Suggested methods of establishing the base value are as follows:

1. If the original cost and year of purchase are available, values can be trended from cost tables to current prices. In the case of a relatively new library, original purchase records may be readily available.

2. An inventory can be made by the librarian or an assistant, and each item or each group of items priced from current catalogs. Frequently, the librarian who purchases the equipment is best able to price such items.

3. The most expensive but also most reliable and effective method is a professional appraisal prepared with detailed itemization by an appraisal company.

Installation costs for communications equipment which is not a part of the building value and for EDP equipment should be included.

The depreciation factor for furniture, fixtures, and equipment is closely related to the expected "life" of the property, that is, the period of time it might be expected to serve its intended purpose. Rugs or carpeting expected to wear out in twenty years may be depreciated 50 percent after ten years. Depreciation for office machines may involve an additional factor, that of obsolescence. For example, a manual typewriter in good condition and with considerably more than half its life remaining may be 75 percent depreciated. Supporting this evaluation may be a substantial supply of used machines available at 25 percent of the original cost.

One additional factor affecting depreciation for certain types of property is the cost of renovation. If a specific item not subject to obsolescence can be placed in a "like new" condition at 25 percent of its replacement (new) cost, 25 percent may be an appropriate depreciation factor.

APPRAISALS AND VALUATION   21

E. **BOOKS AND LIBRARY MATERIALS**

The most difficult valuation problem is that of books and library materials even though these fall within the area of specialization of the librarian. The total number of items involved is so great that an individual pricing as in the case of furniture and fixtures is not practical. The solution comes in developing an average value for each category. Generally, the greater the number of categories into which the library's collection can be divided, the more accurate and reliable will be the final value.

1. *Source of values.* Unfortunately the sources of such average values cannot always be relied upon. The American Library Association has, in the past, developed estimated average values, but these have not been reviewed or renewed in recent years. The *Bowker Annual* (*The Bowker Annual of Library and Book Trade Information.* New York: Bowker, 1956– .) gives average prices for various categories of volumes, but there are several deficiencies in these as a basis for valuation.
    a. The list prices of the newly published volumes may not be based on the same "mix" of books in each category as exists in a given library.
    b. An adjustment must be made for the discount available to the library.
    c. The cost of processing is not included in these prices.
    d. The *Bowker Annual* average prices for the books published in the current year are not entirely applicable because only a small portion of each library's books have been purchased in that year.

    Obviously, the *Bowker Annual* data may be of limited help for special libraries. Librarians in the professions such as law, medicine, and engineering may get assistance directly from publishers in those fields. They may be justified, also, in relying on their own purchase records.

2. *Adjustment of* Bowker Annual *figures.* A number of solutions have been suggested:
    a. The *Bowker Annual* average prices for the last three or four years might represent a figure more appropriate for a given library. However, consideration must be given to the fact that a substantial number of new books are reprints or new editions of older volumes which have been repriced.
    b. Adjustments may be made in the *Bowker Annual* figures for certain local situations where the mix of books is different from that

on which the Bowker average is based. This adjustment might raise or lower average prices.

 c. Over a period of several years, librarians who wish to analyze their own purchases may be able to rely on their own average costs or make adjustment in the *Bowker Annual* costs based on their purchases.

3. *Summary of procedures to be used in pricing.* An annual review should be made to determine the total number of items in each category of books and library materials to apply appropriate average prices to each. Normally, this will entail an adjustment of the previous year's inventory by additions and deletions. Consideration should be given to:

 a. The *Bowker Annual* prices for the past several years compared with any price statistics which the librarian has accumulated

 b. Average discounts being realized by the library in its purchases

 c. Cost of processing each volume (this can be based on either the library's actual cost or the current charges by an outside service, depending on where processing might be done following a serious loss)

 d. Separate pricing for catalog and shelflist cards if they are to be separately insured (as under the Special Library policy or the Valuable Papers form [*see* chap. 5, E.2 and E.3])

 e. Pricing other library materials on a replacement cost basis if they are to be insured for replacement cost

 f. Reducing the value of books and library materials by a depreciated factor if they are to be insured on the actual cash value rather than the replacement cost basis

 g. Reducing the total value by an amount representing the estimated value of books and library materials out on loan (except under the Hartford library form. *See* chap. 5, E.3.c).

F. OTHER TANGIBLE PROPERTY

In any major loss adjustment, it is a great advantage to the library to be able to demonstrate to the company loss adjuster that careful thought and study was given to the subject of values before the insurance was written. This is true for the major categories discussed above and for special types of property, as well.

 A value should be shown in the total valuation summary for every significant category. Supplies and materials should be included even though the value is only an estimate. For leased equipment where the library has responsibility for loss, values agreed to by the owner are desirable. Installation, electrical wiring, and set-up costs also should be included.

In every case where the library assumes or incurs responsibility for property of others it should endeavor to get agreed values from the owners. Courts have frequently hesitated to enforce a exculpatory clause or waiver in favor of a bailee, but generally they have sustained an agreement as to value in the event of loss.

Fine arts, original sculpture or paintings, rare books, and similar materials which have no readily determinable market or replacement value should be priced by a professional in the field (this may be a librarian for rare books, manuscripts, and other rare or irreplaceable library materials and a local art dealer for original paintings, sculptures, etc.). When an item is irreplaceable and there is no ready market for similar items, the value may be purely arbitrary and may depend on whether the proposed value is reasonable and how much premium the library is willing to pay for insurance. By insuring such items on a "valued" policy or form, the insurance company accepts the stated value as the amount of loss if the item is stolen or destroyed.

5

INSURANCE COVERAGES, POLICIES, AND POLICY FORMS

A. IN GENERAL

Insurance on libraries has always been considered "good business" and as a result most insurance companies treat libraries as a preferred class and as eligible for "package" policies and maximum rate credits. Usually one insurance company will insure the entire risk. (There may be an exception where the library is in a very old, highly combustible building, under poor public fire protection, or heavily exposed by surrounding properties.)

The "package" policy may include a variety of insurance coverages, depending on the underwriting practices of the particular company. Usually there is considerable flexibility and substantial premium savings with the package. The premium is the sum of the individual coverage premiums to which a package policy credit is applied. However, there may be instances where separate policies in different companies and written through different agents and brokers are more economical and more desirable than a single package policy.

B. BLANKET PROPERTY—BUILDINGS AND CONTENTS

Blanket coverage (*see* "Blanket form" in Glossary) is usually desirable because it permits various classes of properties at various locations to be included in a single policy with a single amount of insurance. This relieves the library of the risk of being underinsured on some items and overinsured on others because improper values may have been assigned to the various properties.

    1. The blanket policy becomes available by a filing of a statement of values with the insurance company or the rating bureau. The statement of values contains the library's estimate of value of each building and of the contents in each building and is for the purpose of determining an average rate for the blanket policy. Insurance is required to be written with 90 percent coinsurance clause (*see* "Coinsurance" in Glossary) that is, with insurance to 90 percent of the total value. Values may be on a replacement cost basis or an actual cash value basis.

2. When new buildings or new properties are added, a supplementary statement of values may be filed and the policy extended to include new locations. Except for such changes, the values need be filed only at the beginning of the policy, and policies can be written for a three-year term.

3. The property covered may include any or all of the following:
   a. Buildings and structures
   b. Improvements and betterments (in leased building)
   c. Contents, that is,
      (1) Furniture, fixtures, equipment and supplies
      (2) Books and library materials

4. Perils (*refer* to chap. 3, sec. B) insured in the basic form include fire and extended coverage. Additional perils may also be included and coverage is usually available on the "all risks" basis. The standard forms usually contain a $50 or $100 deductible per loss for perils of extended coverage, although the deductible for vandalism and certain other perils may be higher.

C. THE PUBLIC AND INSTITUTIONAL PROPERTY (P.I.P.) FORM

The P.I.P. form is available to libraries subject to a minimum annual premium, usually $500. This is a blanket form, described in section B of this chapter. It has certain advantages over the standard blanket form, although the minimum deductible per loss is $100.

1. The premium is reduced by additional rate credits. The plan contemplates regular fire inspections by the owner (the library insurance agent should be willing to assist in this) on forms furnished by the rating bureau.

2. The obligation of the coinsurance clause can be waived by a special endorsement known as the "Amount of Insurance Clause" (also referred to as the "Agreed Amount Clause"). The library is required to file a statement of values with the rating bureau (or the insurance company) each year and adjust the amount of insurance to at least 90 percent of the total values, at which point the amount of insurance clause becomes effective for 12 months. If values increase

during the year because of additions or inflation, the library will have avoided the risk of a coinsurance penalty due to underinsurance.

3. The policy form covers newly acquired locations, subject to limits of the lesser of 5 percent of the policy or $100,000, with a six-month reporting requirement.

4. The basic form includes perils of fire and extended coverage. Other perils, such as vandalism and sprinkler leakage, as well as the so-called "all risks," can be added by endorsement.

Some insurance companies use specially designed forms which will be known by a name or designation applied by the company. Generally, the forms will be of the blanket type, often slightly broader in coverage than the so-called standard forms described above. In every case the perils covered and the exclusions should be carefully reviewed.

D. SPECIAL PROPERTY ENDORSEMENTS

A number of endorsements are available to modify the standard policy forms when necessary to meet the library's insurance needs.

1. *Contingent liability.* When a building does not conform to current building codes of a municipality so that replacement or repair of fire damage might require a more expensive type of construction, a special endorsement known as "Contingent Liability from Operation of Building Laws" will be available. This will insure the additional cost of repairs made to upgrade the building to comply with the code.

2. *Large deductibles.* Higher deductibles are usually available at additional premium savings. Some special insurance company forms include higher deductibles. These may be attractive to larger libraries. A library with a $200,000 budget can readily accept $250 or $500 when experience indicates it is not likely to have more than one or two losses in any year. Similarly, with a $5,000,000 budget a $5,000 or $10,000 deductible may be acceptable. Whether a higher deductible is desirable will depend on the financial position of the library as well as the amount of rate credit.

3. *Replacement cost.* The standard fire (property) policy insures only to the extent of "actual cash value" (*see* in Glossary) and depreciation may be deducted in arriving at the loss settlement. When the

library feels it cannot or does not wish to suffer a depreciation penalty in the settlement of a loss, it may insure on a replacement cost basis with no deduction for depreciation. This coverage may be included by endorsement in any of the blanket forms described above at no increase in rate (although the premium will be higher because of increased value). This will apply to the entire item of insurance, so that if replacement recovery is desired on buildings and fixtures and equipment only and not on books and library materials, separate amounts of insurance must be designated for the two categories.

Entering into the decision as to replacement cost coverage will be the fact that replacement cost recovery is allowed only if the property destroyed or damaged is actually replaced. Generally, the library and its facilities must be replaced, and since funds to fill the void of depreciation are not usually available, the decision is a simple one. If the property is not to be replaced, loss adjustment must be on an "actual cash value" basis. The same reasoning applies to books and materials. Books common to the typical public library collection are not available on the "used book" market to a significant extent. In event of damage or destruction, replacement will be highly desirable. Such replacement will be at "new," not "used," prices and replacement cost coverage will be required to properly cover the loss. However, this may not be true of certain special collections, such as law books. Because of the continual merging of law firms, there is an active market in used law reports and legal reference books. It may be appropriate for a law library to value some books at new prices and others at "used" market prices. A special policy endorsement can provide for loss settlement at replacement cost (new) or at the cost of used books where available.

4. *Special pricing.* For libraries which are highly valued for their research facilities quite a different problem exists. The lost volumes not only may be very important in the library's operation, they also may be irreplaceable. If the volumes are damaged—for example, water-soaked but not destroyed—they may be salvaged and made usable even through badly scarred. If they cannot be made usable the library's alternative may be to microfilm or microfiche copies of the damaged books borrowed from another library. In this event, it would seem reasonable to value such volumes at the cost of copying and to endorse the policy to provide for recovery on this basis.

Some policies exclude coverage for certain types of property and for loss by certain perils. The library may want to eliminate these exclusions by special endorsement. The insurance agent or consultant should review these limitations in light of the library's needs.

E. BOOKS AND LIBRARY MATERIALS

Three methods of insuring books and library materials are commonly employed. Each has advantages and disadvantages although any one of the three, if properly used, can provide acceptable coverage for the library.

1. *Blanket Contents* form. Under this coverage books and library property may be treated as contents, together with furniture, fixtures, and equipment, and insured under the blanket policy form or the P.I.P. form. Many companies will insure books and library materials on a replacement cost basis, subject to the standard limitation that replacement cost is not recoverable unless the property is actually replaced. If not replaced the loss will be paid on the basis of the actual cash value (depreciated value). The 90 percent coinsurance clause will apply, and the "Amount of Insurance" clause will be available. (*Refer to* secs. B.1 and C.2 in this chapter.) Loss settlement is usually made on the basis of the value of each individual book destroyed, although the adjuster and the library may agree to an average value per volume when a large number of volumes are involved.

2. *Valuable Papers* form. Historically, books and library materials have been separately insured as "valuable papers," presumably because physically they are "papers" and psychologically they are "valuable." Actually they are more akin to merchandise or equipment and are logically insured with other contents as described above. However, there are certain advantages to coverage under the valuable papers form, as well as disadvantages:

   a. It provides very broad coverage, being "all risk" without the usual insurance exclusions of flood and earthquake
   b. It is not subject to a coinsurance clause
   c. The form requires that the insured declare unit values for various classes of property. This restriction can be a serious limitation at the time of loss settlement.
   d. Loss settlement is limited to actual cash value; that is, depreciation will be deducted for books and materials which are not new.

If the insurance company will agree to a modification of the Valuable Papers form to cover "replacement cost for items actually replaced" and to provide a single amount of insurance on a blanket basis (that is, without the limit of a price per item for various categories of books and library materials) the library will have the "best of both worlds."

3. *Special library policy.* This special policy form on a "valued" basis, subject to annual reporting, was developed by Gage-Babcock and Associates in collaboration with a committee of the American Library Association and the Hartford Fire Insurance Company. The model form (*see* in *Protecting the Library and its Resources: A Guide to Physical Protection and Insurance* [Chicago: Library Technology Project, American Library Assn., 1963], pp. 175–208), with minor modifications, has been accepted by a number of insurance carriers and is generally known as the Hartford library policy.

   a. This policy form requires a statement of values to be filed each year which lists the quantity and price per volume or per unit for various categories of books and library materials.
   b. Loss of books and library materials is settled on the basis of the declared values without regard to the actual value or replacement value of the individual items destroyed.
   c. There is a "full reporting clause" which has the effect of a 100 percent coinsurance clause. That is, if values are reported at less than the correct value at the time of reporting, any loss settlement is reduced proportionately.
   d. Coverage is on an "all risk" basis, including earthquake and flood, although the latter is limited to 20 percent of the amount of the policy, or $100,000, whichever is smaller.
   e. Policy covers all property, wherever situated, including property in transit. A $250 deductible applies for each loss which would effectively bar recovery of losses of books in the hands of individual borrowers.
   f. Policy includes "Impairment of Services" coverage—a form of extra expense insurance.

   The policy may include furniture, fixtures, tools, and equipment which are insured on a replacement cost basis; improvements and betterments insured on the basis of sound (actual cash) value; and fine arts which must be scheduled in the policy at specified values.

4. *Recommendation.* Any of the three forms should adequately cover the risks of loss involved. The blanket form allows for the greatest

flexibility because the library is not committed to nor limited to a specific value on each book or category of books nor to a total value of all books and library materials. The policy limitation applies to the entire property value, including building and contents. In both of the other two forms, the amount of insurance applies only to books and library materials. If these are accurately valued there is no disadvantage in these forms.

The final decision as to form to be adopted by the library will depend in part on the following:

a. Whether coverage for earthquake and flood is important, in which case one of the valued forms may be most desirable
b. Whether recovery for loss shall be on the basis of an average value for each volume in a given category as declared in the policy without regard to the replacement value of any individual volume (Hartford Special Library form) or on an actual cash value basis (Valuable Papers form) or on a replacement cost basis (Blanket Contents form)
c. Whether the library is willing to rely on its annual report of values as being wholly accurate and adequate for loss settlement (Hartford form) or prefers to rely on its total insurance for buildings and contents as satisfying the 90 percent coinsurance clause (blanket form) but without a specific limit per unit or in total for all books and library materials.

F. LARGE DEDUCTIBLE (SELF-RETENTION) PLANS

Very large libraries, or those connected with large institutions, which can assume the first $100,000 of each loss will find a special insurance market with especially attractive premiums. Coverage will usually be in a separate policy not a part of the so-called "package" policy and on one of two forms. It may be on the standard blanket form with limit or amount of liability at 90 percent of total values. The total risk will usually be shared by several companies.

An alternative is the "layer" basis in which one or more companies assume all loss in excess of the self-retention up to a specific limit—say $1,000,000. A second layer may cover $4,000,000 in excess of the first $1,000,000, and a third, $10,000,000 in excess of $5,000,000. The institution is then covered for a total of $15,000,000 per loss in excess of its retention. This total limit will usually be agreed upon as the maximum probable loss. Premium will be predicated usually on total values and will be substantially less for the higher layers. Even though values are 50 or 100 million dollars, the limit per loss at 10 or 15 million dollars may be adequate if properties are well protected, of fire resistive construction, or well dispersed.

If the institutional financial structure justifies a vastly higher deductible than the library, an aggregate deductible fund may be reserved by the institution enabling it to charge only a small portion of the self-retention for any loss to the library or other division. In the above example, assume the institution's total annual budget is $50,000,000 and the library's, $2,500,000. The latter might be assessed only $2,500 or $5,000 per loss by the institution which absorbs the balance of the $100,000 deductible in its aggregate deductible fund.

G. MISCELLANEOUS PROPERTY COVERAGES

1. *Fine arts* are appropriately insured under a "valued policy," that is, with a scheduled value for each item which value will be the basis of loss settlement. This may be in a separate policy or it may be an endorsement to a package policy. The values may be the original costs or the value determined by a recognized appraiser. (For fine arts on loan to the library, refer to item no. 3 in this section.)

2. *Valuable records* may also be covered under a separate policy or by a special endorsement to a package policy. These valuable records will not normally include books and library materials nor inventory lists for such items, but they will include special records which have an intangible value involving substantial expenditure to duplicate. The Hartford form is designed to include such special values as the library's option.

   The P.I.P. form includes, without charge, coverage of 1 percent of the policy amount, not exceeding $5,000, on valuable records. (The library is advised to microfilm its shelflist rather than insure it as "valuable records." *See also* chap. 8, sec. J, "Microfilming the Shelflist.")

   It is important to note that most property (fire) insurance forms limit loss recovery on written and printed records to the cost of the paper plus cost of transcribing and on magnetic tapes or discs to the value of the unexposed tape or disc. Valuable records insurance is desirable when it may be necessary to search out information which has been lost. The insurance recovery may involve labor, travel expense, postage, office expense, and the like.

3. *Bailee liability* is appropriate where the library holds personal property of others (such as items on exhibit) on which it has no agree-

ment relating to insuring of the property and where it is not concerned about insuring the interest of the owner. The premium may be much lower if it insures only its legal liability as a bailee. Coverage may be under a separate policy or by an endorsement to a package policy.

If the library desires to insure the entire loss to the property including the interest of the owner, it should include such property in its declaration of contents under its blanket policy form and it should agree in writing with the owner that it will insure owner's interest. At the same time, it should secure a commitment from the owner as to the value of the property.

4. *Transportation floater.* Under the Hartford form the values of all books and library materials must be reported annually and they are insured against "all risks" wherever situated. Coverage will apply to property at outside locations as well as to property in transit.

   The standard valuable papers form extends coverage to apply up to 10 percent of the amount of the policy, not exceeding $5,000, to property in transit and temporarily at other locations.

   The P.I.P. form does not cover property in transit but does cover personal property while temporarily at other locations within the state, up to 1 percent of the amount of the policy, not exceeding $5,000. Property such as books and library materials in transit are subject to perils not normally covered under the blanket building and contents policy and are more appropriately covered under a transportation floater policy or endorsement designed for contents in transit. This form is especially appropriate for books and library materials which are regularly in transit as in bookmobiles.

5. *Plate glass.* The blanket building policy will cover breakage of glass from perils of fire and extended coverage. However, it will not cover accidental breakage, breakage from unknown causes, nor from vandalism. If plate glass is to be insured for such breakage, it must be specifically insured. Usually this requires a listing of each plate. Coverage may be provided by endorsement to a package policy or by a separate policy. Certain insurance companies write plate glass insurance on a 50/50 basis, charging 50 percent of the premium initially and the balance as losses occur within the policy year.

6. *Steam boiler explosion* must be specifically insured either in a separate policy or by endorsement to a package. Coverage may be broadened to include "breakdown." As in the case of fire insurance, coverage is available on a "replacement cost" basis. (For an ex-

planation of the inspection service available by the insurers, *refer to* chap. 3, E.3, "Steam boiler.")

7. *Burglary and theft* of personal property usually are not covered in blanket building and contents forms, even on the "all risk" basis. If a substantial amount is subject to loss, it may be desirable to write separate coverage on such property. This can be as a separate contract or may be added by endorsement to a package policy.

    The principles of risk management are especially appropriate in this area. (*Refer to* chap. 8, "Loss Prevention, Protection, and Safety.") The amount of probable loss is usually not great enough to justify the purchase of insurance.

8. *Money and securities* must be insured separately, also. Usually the library can limit the money on hand so that insurance is not necessary. The risk of loss to any securities it owns can usually be transferred to a bank or other financial institution to which the securities may be surrendered for safekeeping.

9. *Flood insurance* is generally not available from the insurance companies for buildings nor for contents, except under some special forms such as the valuable papers form and the Hartford library policy.

    Recently a national flood insurance program has been made available by the U.S. Department of Housing and Urban Development. The program applies only to communities which have been declared eligible for coverage by HUD. New communities are being declared eligible from time to time. A local insurance agent can determine whether your community is eligible and can quote rates and premiums under the program.

    The flood insurance policy is limited in amount and is not subject to endorsement or modification. It excludes loss by surface waters and backing up of sewers, unless these result from flood conditions.

10. *Difference in (of) conditions* (D.I.C. or D.O.C.) describes a type of policy providing broader coverage for larger libraries, usually those in the multimillion dollar category and especially those which are a part of a large institution. Such libraries may find it practical to insure their properties on a standard building and contents form for fire and extended coverage and to purchase a separate policy with a lower limit and a higher deductible for additional perils. This policy is usually written without a coinsurance clause, although the premium may be based on total values at risk. It is "all risk" but specifically excludes perils covered under the basic or standard policy.

The D.I.C. (or D.O.C.) policy will also exclude the so-called uninsurable risks of wear and tear, mechanical breakdown, war, and the like. It may cover flood and earthquakes, subject to a higher deductible and a lower limit than other losses under the policy, depending upon the circumstances and location of the property. The relatively high deductible with D.I.C. or D.O.C. coverage permits a very low premium. The policy conforms to the risk management philosophy of insuring remote catastrophe risks if the premium is reasonable.

H. COMPREHENSIVE PUBLIC LIABILITY

Comprehensive public liability coverage may be in a separate policy or as part of a package. It will include both bodily injury and property damage liability for accidents arising out of the library activities, including ownership and occupancy of premises, operations, elevator liability, independent contractors, and products liability.

1. Suggested *limits of liability* will vary according to the geographic location, population concentration, size of the library and business practice in the community. In our changing society, limits considered reasonable five years ago must now be doubled or tripled. Minimum limits which the library should accept are:

Bodily injury: $100,000 for injury to one person
$300,000 for injuries arising out of one accident
Property damage: $50,000 for damage per accident.

The typical public library, unless it has umbrella coverage of $1,000,000 or more, should raise its basic limits to $500,000 or $1,000,000.

2. It is advantageous to cover *employees as additional insureds*. The standard liability policy protects the library as well as individual directors, trustees, and officers. For a modest additional premium it can be extended to include employees as additional insureds. Such coverage is important because in most liability claims which are based on negligence, the individual employee who committed the negligent act may be equally liable with the employer. The employee normally does not have insurance under his or her personal insurance policies for business risks; therefore, he or she should be covered as an additional insured under the library policy.

3. *Personal injury* endorsement should be added, for which coverage premium charge is modest. This will extend the liability policy to cover certain torts in addition to bodily injury. (*Refer to* chap. 3, C.2, "Personal injury.")

4. *Contractual liability* is covered to a limited extent in the standard policy. Blanket contractual liability endorsement will broaden the coverage and cost will be modest. (*Refer to* chapter 3, D.3, "Contracts.")

5. *Products liability* applies to the liability which might arise out of an injury caused by a product which is distributed to members of the public. This has relatively little application to a library's normal operation, but it could involve a risk where food is dispensed and consumed off the premises, resulting in injury. The premium charge for the coverage is nominal.

6. *Dram shop liability* may be a necessity in certain instances. Some state statutes provide that anyone injured by an intoxicated person shall have a direct action against the one who served liquor to such person. Accordingly some liability policies exclude dram shop liability. Although the statutes are intended to apply to sale of liquor, court cases have indicated that the statutes may apply to hosts such as one serving his friends or customers or employees. Host liquor liability coverage is generally available in these situations at a modest cost and should be considered by libraries serving liquor at meetings or receptions.

7. Coverage for *property of others* should be obtained in some cases. The property damage portion of the public liability policy excludes liability for damage to property rented to, used by, or in the care, custody, or control of the insured. Fire legal liability coverage is intended to cover the catastrophe risk of liability for fire damage to a building which a library leases from another. The risk arises when an owner or its insurer (through subrogation, for definition of which *see* Glossary) makes claim against the library for an allegedly negligent fire. This coverage should be provided unless a legally binding release can be secured from the owner of leased premises. Coverage may be extended to apply to certain additional perils, also. (For insurance covering liability for personal property, *refer to* chap. 5, G.3, "Bailee liability.")

I. AUTO LIABILITY

1. *Owned vehicles* licensed for highway use should be insured for liability with limits at least as high as recommended above for comprehensive public liability and property damage, namely,

Bodily injury: $100,000 for injury to one person
$300,000 for injuries arising out of one accident
Property damage: $50,000 for damage per accident.

If there is to be no umbrella liability coverage, a minimum of $500,000 or $1,000,000 single limit should be provided for bodily injury and property damage under the auto policy. The standard auto policy will cover the library, as well as anyone for whom the library is acting and any person driving library vehicles with the library's permission.

2. *Physical damage* insurance generally known as "comprehensive fire and theft and collision coverage" should be included. For ordinary vehicles a $100 deductible collision is standard. For expensive units such as a bookmobile, a higher deductible may be justified by savings in premium. A large library or institution with a fleet of vehicles may be justified in accepting a higher deductible or even self-insuring all physical damage, except for the catastrophe risk of fire or similar damage if many vehicles are stored at a single location.

3. The library is subject to additional risk known as *non-owned auto liability*. Under the legal doctrine of respondeat superior, an employer is responsible for the torts of his employee committed in the course of his/her duties. This means that a page who is sent to the hardware store by the librarian and drives his/her own car will incur a liability on behalf of the library if an accident occurs. This applies even though the employee may be prohibited by library rules from driving a privately owned car. If the employee has auto liability insurance, the library will be covered under the employee's policy. However, the employee may have inadequate or no insurance. To protect itself against such a contingency, the library needs non-ownership coverage. This can include liability for "hired cars." The premium for non-ownership coverage is modest. It is important that library employees understand that this coverage does not protect them personally.

If the library owns licensed vehicles, a comprehensive liability and physical damage policy will cover all of the aforementioned exposures to risk. If it owns no vehicles, the auto non-ownership risk will usually be added by endorsement to the comprehensive public liability or the package policy.

J. **UMBRELLA (EXCESS) LIABILITY**

Umbrella liability coverage is written as a separate policy to apply as excess over the primary liability policies (comprehensive public liability and auto liability) in multiples of $1,000,000. For small public libraries for whom the policy minimum premium of $300 to $500 is large in relation to the insurance budget, it may be possible for the municipality to add the library as additional insured to its policy for a nominal additional premium. Limits of $2,000,000 and $5,000,000 are not uncommon for public properties or where large groups may be assembled. Institutional risks are now purchasing even higher limits.

Usually the umbrella policy will be broader than the underlying (or primary) general liability and auto liability policies. Claims which come under the umbrella but which are not covered by the primary policies are subject to a self retention (or deductible) which may vary from $5,000 to $25,000.

K. EMPLOYEE DISHONESTY BOND

Some state statutes require a "qualifying bond" for the treasurer as well as for other officers of the library board. This is a guarantee of "faithful performance" by the person bonded. It includes the risk of dishonesty. The principal dishonesty risk, however, may exist among unnamed employees. A loss may result from collusion with outsiders for theft of library property, or with suppliers who agree to shortages in shipments, to overpayment of invoices, or of invoices for goods not received. The proper coverage for the employee dishonestry risk is a blanket bond covering all employees without naming them. Two blanket forms are available, one with a limit applying to each employee involved in the defalcation, the other with a limit per loss.

An appropriate limit under either form will depend on the size of the library and its financial controls. A limit of 10 to 20 percent of the annual budget may be appropriate for a small library and a limit as low as 1 to 2 percent for the very large institution.

L. EXTRA EXPENSE FOR RESUMPTION OF OPERATIONS

The Hartford library policy includes extra expense coverage to the extent of 15 percent of the amount of property insurance. This is described as "impairment of services" coverage. Some special package policies of other companies will include nominal amounts without charge. Additional amounts are available by endorsement to the property policies or in a separate policy. (*Refer to* chap. 3, E.6, "Extra Expense.")

M. WORKERS' COMPENSATION

Workers' compensation must be written as a separate policy. The coverage is mandatory in most states and limits are statutory. Premium is based on payroll and the policy is subject to audit at its expiration. The library may be justified in combining its coverage with another organization in certain situations:

1. Where employees are common to two organizations (e.g., a system and a library), it may be difficult to determine which was the employer at the moment of injury. To avoid a controversy between insurance companies, a single policy, or policies, in the same company may be desirable.

2. In the case of a library which has arranged for the municipality to handle its funds, issue payroll checks, and perform payroll bookkeeping, it may be desirable to include the library coverage with the municipality. The library directors should require that,
   a. The library's board of directors be named as additional insured, and
   b. A certificate of insurance be issued to the library as evidence that insurance is in force.

In the states of Nevada, North Dakota, Ohio, Washington, West Virginia, and Wyoming this insurance must be purchased from the state fund. In all other states, coverage is normally provided by private insurance companies. In those instances where the workmen's compensation statute is not mandatory, the library should elect to come within the act if it can. This will guarantee benefits to employees injured on the job and will bar a common law action for injuries.

N. DIRECTORS', OFFICERS', TRUSTEES' LIABILITY

There are three forms of coverage which may be applicable depending upon the nature of the library's legal status, that is, whether it is a nonprofit corporation, a part of a governmental body, or a public school district. The coverages being considered here are not included nor generally available in the standard public liability insurance policy. Relatively few insurance companies provide these special coverages and usually policies must be ordered through an excess or surplus lines broker.

1. *Directors', Officers', and Trustees' form* is most appropriate for the private, nonprofit corporation or organization. Coverage applies to

6

NEW CONSTRUCTION

A. IN GENERAL

New construction projects create new and unusual risks for the library but they afford an opportunity to apply the conecpts of risk management to the library's advantage.

Cooperation between the architect and the insurance agent or consultant before the plans are finalized may help to reduce fire hazards and make the premises safer. Delineating insurance requirements for the contractor will shift the risk of claims for accidents to the one whose activity is likely to have caused those accidents.

The insurance considerations discussed in this chapter may apply to remodeling and maintenance contracts as well as major construction projects.

B. INSURANCE REVIEW OF ARCHITECT'S PLANS

The architect is aware of and generally familiar with building and safety code requirements. He may not be familiar with underwriting and insurance rating-bureau requirements necessary to secure the most favorable insurance rates. He should be urged to seek the cooperation of the library's insurance agent or consultant (and/or the insurance company engineer) and to have rating bureau or insurance company review and approval of his plans (*see* chap. 7, A, "Property (Fire) Insurance Rating").

The architect's specifications (general conditions section) which designate the insurance requirements both for liability for accidents and loss or damage to the property (builders' risk) should also be reviewed by the library's insurance representative prior to construction.

C. THE HOLD HARMLESS CLAUSE

An indemnity (hold harmless) clause should be made a part of the construction contract. Because the owner (library) is usually liable liability for "wrongful act" which is usually defined as "any actual or alleged error or misstatement or misleading statement or act or omission or neglect or breach of duty by the Directors, Officers or Trustees in the discharge of their duties, or any matter claimed against them solely by reason of their being Directors, Officers or Trustees of the organization." This is generally construed to include violations of civil and constitutional rights, although the policy will apply only to directors, officers, or trustees and will not defend employees who are not officers. There are numerous exclusions, including the personal injury liability risks which can be separately insured under the general liability policy: liability resulting from failure to purchase insurance; liability for fraudulent or dishonest acts; and liability for acts resulting in personal gain. When the corporation or public institution (i.e., the library) has adopted a bylaw provision for indemnifying officers and directors for liability for these acts, the policy will also provide insurance for the corporation or public institution.

2. *Public Officials' Liability policy* provides similar coverage and will be appropriate for municipally-owned and other public libraries. Coverage applies to liability for "wrongful act," defined essentially the same as in the directors', officers', and trustees' policy. Usually it can be extended to include employees as insureds. This may be especially important to librarians and others in a supervisory capacity because it may present the only opportunity to provide coverage for these persons for civil and constitutional rights violations.

3. *Board of Education Liability* or *Public School Trustees' Liability* may be available for libraries which are part of a public school system. It may usually be extended to insure library employees.

Policies such as the foregoing will usually contain a deductible or (insured's) retention clause and they may also require a small participation (usually 5 percent) to be paid by the insured in event of loss. The policies are on a "claims made" basis, that is, the policy covers claims made or first discovered during the term of the policy. This is in contrast with other liability policies which provide coverage if the accident or act complained of occurred during the policy term, even though claim is made after the policy has expired.

for accidents on its premises when hazardous work is being performed, the indemnity clause is necessary to shift the responsibility for injuries back to the contractor who has charge of the work.

D. INSURANCE REQUIREMENTS FOR THE CONTRACTOR

The contractor should be required to furnish certificate of insurance before commencing construction for:

1. Workers' compensation
2. Comprehensive general liability including (a) contractual liability (insuring the indemnity clause referred to above) and (b) completed operations (applying to accidents occurring as a result of defects in the structure after completion)
3. Comprehensive auto liability.

Policy limits required will depend on those customary for the type of work in the area.

E. OWNERS' PROTECTIVE LIABILITY INSURANCE

A contingent liability coverage known as owners' protective liability is designed to protect the owner in the event there is a question as to whether an accident arose out of the construction project (and, therefore, is within the indemnity agreement). Some construction contracts will require the contractor to furnish an owners' protective policy in the name of the library. More logically the library will purchase this coverage as a part of its comprehensive public liability policy, in which case the coverage will be described as "independent contractor's coverage." The premium is modest and is based on the amount of the contract.

F. SURETY (PERFORMANCE) BOND

Public bodies generally are required by statute to secure a bond from the contractor guaranteeing performance of the contract, usually in the amount of the contract. This is protection against insolvency during the job but also against the risk of liens which might be levied against the property for work or materials of subcontractors and suppliers whom the contractor has failed to pay.

Private libraries and institutions also are well advised to consider the protection of such a bond even though the premium cost will increase the contract price.

G. BUILDERS' RISK INSURANCE

Builders' risk insurance covers the building during the course of construction. Since both the builder and the library have an insurable interest in the project during construction, it is most economical to insure both interests in a single policy. The policy may be purchased by the library or the contractor, depending on the contract terms. Its essential features are as follows:

1. Named insured may be the library only or the library and contractor(s). If purchased by the library a suggested wording is "The library and contractors and subcontractors, as their interests may appear, loss, if any to be adjusted with and payable to the named insured (the library)."

2. Amount of coverage is usually the completed value of the building (a rate adjustment is allowed to compensate for the gradual increase in amount at risk).

3. Perils usually include fire and extended coverage but "all risk" coverage is preferable.

4. Deductible in an amount of $500 or $1,000 may be required on the "all risk" form. Usually the deductible will fall on the contractor who has the obligation to protect the property. A specific agreement between the parties on this point is desirable.

The builders' risk policy is intended to apply only during construction and prior to occupancy. If it has not been replaced with permanent insurance at the time of occupancy, the insurance company should be notified.

Where construction involves remodeling of or an addition to an existing building, a builders' risk policy may not be necessary because the blanket building and contents form automatically includes "additions and alterations." If the contract is for a substantial amount, it may be necessary to increase the amount of insurance under the blanket policy as the work progresses.

7

INSURANCE RATES AND PREMIUMS

A. PROPERTY (FIRE) INSURANCE RATES

Fire insurance rates for most insurance companies are established by a state licensed rating bureau, usually the Insurance Services Office (except in the states of Hawaii, Idaho, Louisiana, Mississippi, North Carolina, Texas, and Washington and the District of Columbia). Rates for commercial, industrial and public buildings are based on individual features of construction, occupancy, and protection determined by a personal inspection of each building. It is frequently possible to reduce bureau rates by improvements in construction or protection. With a proper letter of authorization to the rating bureau, the library's insurance agent (or the insurance company engineer) can secure a copy of the rate survey for review and can develop recommendations for rate reductions. (Rates are published in cents per $100 of insurance. For example, a rate of $0.15 will produce a premium of $150 for a $100,000 policy.)

The bureaus will have consultants also who are available to offer advice on improvements as well as on new construction so as to secure the lowest possible rates.

B. WORKERS' COMPENSATION RATES

Rates for workers' compensation are computed annually by occupational category on the basis of actual experience in the state. Libraries will usually have employees in two classes and most states use the following coding to identify them:

> Rating Code 8838—Librarians or professional assistants, including clerical
> Rating Code 9101—All other employees (janitors, drivers, pages, et al).

Rates apply to each $100 of payroll. The initial policy premium

43

is considered a deposit and a final adjustment based on actual payroll is necessary at the expiration of the policy.

When an annual premium exceeds $1,000, experience credits or debits may apply, in addition to a "size of premium" discount. The experience rating will be based on actual losses in relation to premiums for a period of three years immediately preceding the current year.

C.   OTHER INSURANCE CLASSES

Some property rates (e.g., fine arts, valuable papers, extra expense) are based on the individual building or contents fire rates. Liability premiums are based principally on floor areas of library buildings; fidelity bond premiums, on the number of employees; auto, on the kind of vehicle, its location, and its use.

In most cases, insurance companies have some flexibility in rating and where premiums are substantial, actual loss experience of the library will be important.

8

LOSS PREVENTION, PROTECTION, AND SAFETY

A. IN GENERAL

The term "fireproof" is an anomaly when applied to a library building. Contents of libraries are combustible and the most fire resistive structure will suffer heavy damage if a fire continues unchecked. All librarians want their libraries to be safe. Losses no matter how well insured are costly, time-consuming, and frustrating. It is advisable, therefore, that the library utilize all resources reasonably available to prevent loss. Similarly, the librarian should seek to avoid injuries to employees as well as members of the public.

B. INSURANCE COMPANY INSPECTIONS

One of the criteria in choosing an insurance company should be its facilities for inspection service and the competence of its staff in loss control and protection. An agreement should be reached with the insurance company or its agent before a policy is accepted for regular inspections and loss control services.

C. LOCAL FIRE DEPARTMENT INSPECTIONS

Good rapport with the local fire chief is very desirable. He and the firefighters should be given every opportunity to become familiar with the layout of the library building. Periodic inspections by members of the fire department and the librarian or a board member should be encouraged.

D. FIRE PROTECTION STANDARDS

In addition to construction and protection features recommended by the insurance rating bureau and the insurance company, the librarian should have access to the *National Fire Codes* and the standards and recommended practices prepared and published by the National

Fire Protection Association, 470 Atlantic Ave., Boston, MA 02210. Bulletin No. 910 (1970), entitled *Recommended Practice for the Protection of Library Collections from Fire,* discusses past library fires; general principles applying to library building construction, equipment, and facilities; and fire protection equipment.

The most complete treatise to date on physical protection as well as insurance protection for libraries is the ALA Library Technology Project publication entitled *Protecting the Library and Its Resources: A Guide to Physical Protection and Insurance* (LTP pub. no. 7; Chicago: American Library Assn., 1963). A more recent publication dealing with library fires and prevention is *Managing the Library Fire Risk* by John Morris (Berkeley: Univ. of California, 1975). This is available from the Office of Insurance and Risk Management, University of California, 485 University Hall, Berkeley, CA 94720.

E. OUTSIDE PROTECTION AND SECURITY

Even though patrolling by police in the community may provide excellent protection, design of the library building and layout of library grounds can be a serious handicap in preventing vandalism and break-ins. The aesthetic value of beautiful landscaping and soft lights may have to be sacrificed in favor of clear space and spotlights to discourage prowlers.

F. FIRE AND BURGLAR ALARMS

If fire and burglary losses are to be minimized, prompt responses by the fire and police departments are essential. Automatic alarms are effective for this purpose and costs are generally reasonable. Because library insurance premiums are relatively low, premium savings for alarms are not significant in defraying the cost of installations. However, the value of the library's services to its constituents will justify an expenditure for alarms above insurance premium savings.

There is a wide variety of approved fire alarm systems. These may consist of heat or smoke detection units or a combination of both. To be effective a system should cover the entire building. Local bells or sirens should be provided to warn occupants of danger and there should be a direct connection to the fire or police department or a central station. When the library is adjacent to the police or fire station, outside alarm bells may sometimes adequately serve in lieu of a direct wire connection to the station.

Burglar alarms are available in an even wider variety. Where all access points can be "wired," protection may be complete except against a thief who hides in the building at closing time. Light beam or sonic systems may fill this gap. The sophistication of the system should depend on local conditions and experience.

G.   AUTOMATIC SPRINKLERS

Where buildings are of combustible interior construction or the library is large and lacking fire cut-offs, automatic sprinklers are especially desirable. No other form of fire protection approaches their effectiveness. Automatic sprinklers are generally not practical unless city water is available in adequate quantity at adequate pressure and the library is large enough to justify the fairly high cost of getting water into the building. Fire insurance rate credits may run from 50 to 75 percent.

A practical combination of sprinklers and fire alarms can be designed so that there are sprinklers in all areas containing substantial combustible contents and heat and smoke detection devices with central station connection in all other parts of the building.

H.   HALON,® AN EXTINGUISHING AGENT

A relatively recent development in the fire protection field is the use of the gas, Halon,® as an extinguishing agent in areas requiring special protection with a minimum of damage. Its use is especially suitable in confined or properly cut-off areas. It possesses good extinguishing characteristics at a concentration in air which is somewhat below a dangerous level of toxicity.

Halon® gas extinguishing systems are especially desirable for rare book collections where water from sprinklers or fire department hoses might cause irreparable damage.

I.   PROTECTION FROM PILFERAGE

Just as shoplifting is a serious problem in stores, pilfering or stealing of individual books has reached serious proportions in some libraries. Several systems of sensitizing books and library materials are now available for use where personal supervision of the library's patrons and users is not adequate.

Theft insurance will not solve the problem. Insurance is not intended to cover losses of this type and if a series of such losses were presented under a theft policy, the underwriter would insist upon a deductible amount large enough to eliminate coverage on such losses.

J. MICROFILMING THE SHELFLIST

The business of the library is books and the key to the business is the shelflist. No amount of insurance covering that list and few protective devices can equal the value of a duplicate copy stored at another locaion. The shelflist copy is essential as proof of the loss sustained in a catastrophe and it is equally useful as a guide to the librarian in replacing books and materials. Fortunately, microfilming is now available at a reasonable cost. Possession of the film reduces the tangible value of the shelflist cards to a few cents each—the cost of printing. The copy can be updated periodically by filming cards containing additions and deletions.

K. DUPLICATING MAGNETIC TAPES AND DISCS

The proliferation of electronic data processing (EDP) in libraries creates some special problems in protection. As the library increases its use of and therefore its dependency on EDP equipment and magnetic tape or disc for storage of information, it increases its catastrophe risk. Protection systems are available but none is equivalent to duplicating the bulk of the library's records and maintaining the duplicates at a detached location. The duplication process need not be expensive since the parent (previous generation) of each current set of discs or tapes will serve as a duplicate to preserve all but new information.

L. OSHA REQUIREMENTS

The Occupational Safety and Health Act adopted by the federal government in 1970 applies to all employees (except state and local government) with reference to employee injuries. Some states have taken over OSHA responsibilities and may apply the regulations to state and local governmental bodies.

The most important part of this statute for libraries is the maintenance of adequate records relating to on-the-job injuries for employees. Details of this record-keeping are contained in the U.S. Department of Labor booklet entitled "Record-keeping Requirements under the Williams-Steiger Occupational Safety and Health Act of 1970."

9

LOSSES AND CLAIMS

A. IN GENERAL

The insurance agent will be a key person in connection with losses and claims, although cooperation of the library staff is essential. An important part of the insurance program is the assignment of responsibility for reporting losses and accidents which might result in claims. This includes instructions as to how and to whom reports are to be made.

B. PROMPT REPORTING OF LOSSES AND ACCIDENTS

Most policies require that insurer be notified of losses and accidents quickly. This is necessary if claims are to be handled properly.

1. Major property losses. Especially those which the insurance company adjuster may wish to investigate personally, such as fire, explosion, burglary, and the like, should be reported immediately by telephone.

2. Workers' compensation. Coverage requires an "Employer's First Report of Injury" to satisfy the Industrial Commission or other state body responsible for administering workers' compensation benefits.

3. Auto accidents. Most states require that auto accidents must be reported on a standard accident form. The normal time limit is 24 hours from the time of the accident if bodily injury is involved and ten days if only property damage occurs. The state form is usually acceptable to the insurance company.

4. Other liability. All injuries to persons on library premises should be reported if it is reasonable to suspect that a claim might be made for such injuries. It is desirable to discuss the reporting of such incidents with the insurance company or agent or broker in order to develop guidelines to be followed.

C. PROOF OF LOSS

Most property policies require proof of loss to be filed within 60 days, although this requirement may be waived by the insurer. Companies seldom invoke this condition and adjusters usually waive it by their actions, if not directly. However, in any loss where there is a serious question of coverage, the provision should be strictly complied with.

D. COOPERATION WITH THE LIABILITY INSURANCE COMPANY

The liability insurance company steps into the shoes of the library when a claim for injury is presented. It has the right, legally, to full cooperation of the library's personnel in the defense. If there is a clear-cut case of liability, the insurance company will generally be anxious to settle with the claimant. However, settlement is the prerogative of the company and the library should not make any commitments.

Because the insurance company undertakes to handle all aspects of liability and workmen's compensation claims, it is important that all papers and communications which come to the library be passed on promptly to the insurance company. These may include bills, medical reports, claim letters, summons and complaints constituting lawsuits.

E. SALVAGE OPERATIONS

Damage to books resulting from a fire loss usually involves extensive water damage. Sophisticated salvage procedures have been developed which involve deep freezing to prevent mold and vacuum drying. However, whether salvage is practical will depend upon a number of circumstances.

For those books which are very valuable and irreplaceable the library may be willing to accept the salvaged product even though scars of the damage remain. For books which are replaceable, the decision will depend upon the replacement costs as these relate to salvage expense and condition after salvage. Salvage expense should include handling costs, reprocessing, and filing, as well as contract costs for the salvage process.

APPENDIXES

A. SAMPLE RISK MANAGEMENT POLICY STATEMENT FOR THE SMALL OR MEDIUM-SIZED PUBLIC LIBRARY

By appropriate resolution the Board of Trustees of the _____ Public Library has established the following policy in relation to its property and liability insurance program.

1. Responsibility for administering the insurance program shall rest with the librarian.

2a. The librarian shall designate an insurance agent or broker, subject to approval of the Board, to act as risk management consultant and place all insurance coverages. The agent or broker shall secure bids from financially responsible insurance companies periodically and shall be permitted to charge a fee not exceeding the prevailing brokerage commission for insurance placed with a company which does not allow a commission as part of its premium.

2b. (Alternate provision in lieu of 2a.)
The librarian shall designate an insurance consultant (subject to approval of the Board) whose functions shall include establishing an appropriate insurance program, preparing specifications and securing bids for insurance periodically, and reviewing risks of the Library and analyzing its insurance policies.

3. It is the policy of the Board to insure catastrophe risks and to assume minor risks by self insuring or by the use of deductibles where premium savings warrant. It is the desire of the Board to limit aggregate annual self-insured losses to ½ of 1 percent of the annual budget.

4. Insurance on property (except for automotive equipment) shall be purchased on a replacement cost basis without depreciation in the amount of 90 percent of the insurable replacement cost and shall cover perils commonly insured by libraries.

5. Liability insurance shall cover the Library, its board members, and employees as insureds. It shall be written on a comprehensive basis and limits shall be in amounts generally considered to be reasonably adequate in this area.

6. Workers compensation insurance shall be provided for employees.

7. Employee dishonesty insurance shall be provided on a blanket basis with a limit per loss (or per person) of approximately 10 percent of the annual budget.

8. Other kinds of insurance shall be provided for risks which are common to libraries and which can cause serious loss.

9. Liability insurance for directors (or trustees) and officers shall be provided, if available.

10. The librarian shall report all serious losses to the Board promptly.

11. It shall be the duty of the insurance agent or broker (or consultant) to place insurance in companies which are capable of providing loss prevention services and facilities and to arrange for the utilization of these services and facilities by the Library.

12. The librarian and the insurance agent or broker (or consultant) shall report annually to the Board in the month of _____ on the current insurance program including a description of coverages, limits of liability, deductibles and premiums. The report shall also include recommendations if any for preserving and protecting the Library's property, a list of insured and uninsured losses which have occurred during the past year, and an indication of possible risks of loss for which insurance is not currently available or has not been purchased.

Dated_____19____

APPENDIX B   53

B.   SAMPLE RISK MANAGEMENT POLICY STATEMENT FOR THE LARGE PUBLIC LIBRARY OR INSTITUTIONAL LIBRARY

The Board of Trustees of _____
has by appropriate resolution adopted the following policy statement with relation to the purchase of insurance:

1. The insurance program shall be administered by the Executive Librarian (or Treasurer or Comptroller or Business Manager) who shall report annually to the Board in the month of _____ on the status of the insurance program.

2. Insurance shall be purchased when available
   a. To cover major risks of loss to property of the Library in amounts adequate to replace property destroyed or damaged.
   b. To protect the Library, its officers and directors and employees against claims and suits for personal injury and property damage in amounts and limits generally considered to be reasonably adequate for similar institutions in this area.
   c. To protect the officers, directors, and employees against claims for civil and constitutional rights violations and other statutory liabilities; and to protect directors (or trustees) and officers for liabilities while acting in their capacities as such.

3. Insurance shall be placed on a competitive basis subject to bidding at three-year intervals unless special circumstances justify more frequent or less frequent bidding. On the occasion of such bidding the Executive Librarian (or Treasurer or Comptroller or Business Manager) is authorized to engage the services of an insurance consultant for the purpose of analyzing risks and assisting in the preparation of specifications.

4. Coverage shall be placed with financially sound insurance companies enjoying a good reputation in this community and which can provide appropriate loss prevention and claim handling facilities.

5. The Executive Librarian is authorized to accept deductibles and to self insure minor risks where loss experience of the Library and good business judgment indicates that the aggregate loss within the deductible and self insurance program is not likely to exceed 1 percent of the Library's annual budget nor any individual loss, to exceed ½ of 1 percent of the annual Library budget.

Dated_____19_____

C. EXAMPLE OF VALUATION STUDY (NEW LIBRARY FACILITY)

Note: This study was prepared in 1970 for a specific library and is included here for illustrative purposes only. Insurance was written on "replacement cost" basis.

BUILDING

Building Construction (Auditor's report of 6-24-69)		$539,467
Add ½ of Architect's fee (for Supervision only)		20,361
		$559,828
Deduct for insurance exclusions 10%		55,983
		$503,845
Cost change to date from 1968 10%		50,385
Estimated Building Replacement Cost		$554,230

FURNITURE, FIXTURES & EQUIPMENT

Office equipment (Auditor's report)		$ 3,028
Furniture		39,470
Equipment (from misc. expense)		873
		$ 43,371
Equipment purchases since audit		
W. R. Ames	$ 5,120	
W. R. Ames	1,407	
Kanak Elec.	391	
Instr. Sys. Rec. Player	223	
Sjostrom	1,455	
	21,476	
		30,072
		$ 73,443
Cost increase 5%		3,672
		$ 77,115
Vend-A-Copy machine (leased) (estimated value)		2,500
Supplies (office & bldg. maint.) (estimated)		3,000
Property of employees and patrons (estimated)		1,000
Estimated Furniture, Fixtures, Equipment, & Supplies		$ 83,615

BOOKS, RECORDINGS & INVENTORY RECORDS

Adult books 33,399 @ $7.92	$264,500
(Based on *Bowker Annual 1969*, adjusted to exclude children's books and to reflect adult fiction at ⅓ of total)	
Children's books 12, 656 @ $3.47	44,000
	$308,500

APPENDIX C

Less ⅓ estimated average discount	102,800
	$205,700
Processing cost per book 46,055 @ $1.30	60,000
(Includes index card costs)	$265,700
Recordings	1,000
Periodicals @ 3-year cost	6,000
Estimated Replacement Cost	$272,700

D. ANALYSIS OF INSURABLE VALUES

Note: An actual case study, this was prepared for a specific library in 1969 and is included here for illustrative purposes only. Insurance was written on "actual cash value" (depreciated) basis.

BUILDINGS

Building values have been developed from the 1961 Lloyd-Thomas Co. appraisal of the original two-story building and the original 1962–1964 cost of improvements and new addition, all trended to reflect 1969 values. The Lloyd-Thomas Co. insurance depreciation factor in 1961 was 35 percent. This is normally considered to be the maximum building depreciation allowable in this area for a building in good useable condition. The normal insurance depreciation for the rear addition would be about 10 percent and we have applied an average overall factor of 25 percent.

Main building, 1961 Lloyd-Thomas Co. appraisal, replacement cost		$33,400
Cost change to date, 37%		12,350
		$45,750
Basement improvement		1,950
Facade remodeling (consider enhancement in value at ½ of total cost)		2,800
		$50,500
Original cost, rear addition, 1962	$26,000	
Cost increase to date, 35%	9,100	
		35,100
Total building replacement cost, 1969		$85,600
Estimated depreciation 25%		21,900
Building insurable value (actual cash value)		$63,700

FURNITURE AND FIXTURES AND EQUIPMENT AND SUPPLIES

The librarian has reviewed the 1967 inventory sheets, making additions and corrections, and has revised the valuations after spot-checking values of certain items. We believe this is a fairly reliable value for insurance purposes. We believe that insurance adjusters would approve an overall average depreciation factor of 25 percent.

Furniture and fixtures and equipment, per librarian's inventory of 11/17/69 (replacement cost new)	$27,374	
Insurance depreciation 25%	6,844	
Net insurable value (actual cash value)		$20,530
To provide additional coverage for miscellaneous items not inventoried and for consumable supplies, consider replacement cost new value at		$28,500
Depreciated or actual cash value		$21,500

BOOKS, RECORDS, FILMS AND CARDS

On the basis of the book inventory furnished in the librarian's letter of November 17 and based on the Bowker Annual for 1969, we have determined values for each of the classes of books. The Bowker prices are based on list or retail. Your purchases are at an average discount of one-third. We understand that the Processing Center service cost, including all index cards, amounts to $1.30 per volume. The Bowker adult fiction and children's book values have been taken as shown in the table. The nonfiction average value has been revised to eliminate from the average, children's books, adult fiction and certain other very expensive categories of which you have relatively few volumes. These include art, law, medicine, and technology.

Books, adult nonfiction	13,414 @ $8.70	$116,700
Adult fiction	7,407 @ $4.93	36,500
Children's	12,838 @ $3.47	44,600
		$197,800
Less ⅓ estimated average discount		65,900
		$131,900
Processing Center cost per book, including cards	33,659 @ $1.30	43,800
		$175,700
Estimate minimum of 10% of total volumes out on loan at all times, deduct		17,600
		$158,100
Records	$755 less ⅓ discount $500	
Film strips	80	
Microfilm (time)	120	
Periodicals—6-year cost	5,500	
		6,200
Net replacement insurable value		$164,300
Insurance depreciation estimated at 20% (this is a low percentage, justified because of regular procedure for discarding obsolete books)		32,800
Depreciated or actual cash value		$131,500

VALUATION SUMMARY

	Replacement Cost	Actual Cash Value
Buildings	$ 85,600	$ 63,700
Furniture, fixtures, equipment, and supplies	28,500	21,500
Books, records, films, cards	164,300	131,500
Total	$278,400	$216,700

58   *Insurance Manual for Libraries*

E.   SPECIAL LIBRARY POLICY—REPORT OF VALUES

THE HARTFORD INSURANCE GROUP
HARTFORD, CONNECTICUT

Hartford Fire Insurance Company
Hartford Accident and Indemnity Company
Citizens Insurance Company of New Jersey

New York Underwriters Insurance Company
Twin City Fire Insurance Company

Name of Applicant or Insured			Policy Date

Name and Location of Library			As of Inventory Date

Reporting of Values: The following is the agreed value of all property described below, the sound value of improvements paid for by the Insured, and the total replacement cost new of all other insured property at all locations and in transit.

DESCRIPTION OF PROPERTY	QUANTITY	AMOUNT PER ARTICLE		AMOUNT
Adult Fiction		@$	per volume	$
Adult non-Fiction		@$	per volume	$
Juvenile Materials		@$	per volume	$
Reference Books		@$	per volume	$
Periodicals (bound)		@$	per volume	$
Periodicals (not bound)		@$	per volume	$
Bound documents		@$	per volume	$
Unbound documents		@$	per volume	$
Newspapers before 1865		@$	per issue (per volume)	$
Newspapers 1865 to date		@$	per issue (per volume)	$
Micro-Cards (includes all forms of micro print)		@$	per unit	$
Tape recordings		@$	each	$
Sheet music		@$	per sheet	$
Phonograph Records		@$	per record	$
Pamphlets		@$	per piece	$
		@$	per	$
		@$	per	$
Shelf list		@$	per card	$
Adult catalog		@$	per card	$
Juvenile catalog		@$	per card	$
Registration cards		@$	per card	$
Withdrawal cards		@$	per card	$
Microfilm		@$	per reel	$
		@$	per	$
		@$	per	$
			TOTAL	$

Description of Fine Arts* (Pictures, paintings, sculptures, etc.); Manuscripts, rare books and special collections	AMOUNT

Sound value of building improvements paid for by the Insured. . . . . $
Replacement cost new of all other insured property at above location. (Furniture, Fixtures, Tools, Equipment, etc.) . . . $
Replacement cost new of all other insured property in transit. . . . . $
*Fine Arts—Show location of Fine Arts if at other than above location.

Date..   Applicant or Insured..   Signature and Title

Form 11426-1   Printed in U. S. A.   6-'65

APPENDIX F

F. A TYPICAL ANALYSIS OF *BOWKER ANNUAL* PRICES

The 1975 *Bowker Annual* Index Prices (*Publishers Weekly* 209(6):54–59 [9 Feb. 1976]) show an average price per volume for new issues of $16.19. The following adjustments may be necessary to determine appropriate prices for a given library.

1. Removing Fiction and Juveniles (which are separately inventoried by the library) results in a revised average for remaining volumes of $17.72. (Those wishing to be more precise can break Nonfiction into various categories.)

2. It will be noted that over 25 percent of the total new volumes are represented by the special classes of Law, Medicine, and Sociology and Economics, the prices of which average over $21. Assuming that a library has only about 8 percent of its volumes in these classes, the *Bowker Annual* average can be recomputed after eliminating two-thirds of the volumes and costs in these classes. The new average is reduced from $17.72 to about $16.68.

3. Considering the age of the library it may be appropriate to compute similar averages based on 1974 and 1973 *Bowker Annual* prices. For 1974 the averages, excluding Fiction and Juveniles and adjusting the balance for reduced special classes, is $14.84. The 1973 *Bowker Annual* prices indicate the class of Sociology and Economics to be approximately equal to the overall average and it is, therefore, not worthwhile to make the second adjustment.

4. The revised prices for three classes for three years are as follows:

	1975	1974	1973	3-year Avge.
Adult Fiction	8.31	7.43	7.37	7.70
Juvenile	5.82	5.01	4.65	5.16
Nonfiction	16.68	14.84	13.20	14.91

It will be noted that the three-year average is fairly close to the second prior year. A librarian may have the equivalent of a three-year average by utilizing last year's prices for next year's insurance. For example, a study of values during 1976 will be based on 1975 prices, and the amount of insurance arrived at will extend at least part way into 1977.

G. CHECKLIST FOR LIBRARY INSURANCE

PROPERTY	VALUATION DATE	PERILS INSURED
___ Buildings	_____	___ Fire & Extended Cov.
___ Impr. & Bett. (Leased Bldgs.)	_____	___ Vandalism
___ Furn., Fixt., Eqpt. & Supplies	_____	___ Sprinkler Leakage
___ Books & Library Materials	_____	___ Water Damage
___ Property at Other Locations	_____	___ Collapse of Building
___ Property of Others at Library	_____	___ Burglary & Theft
___ Property of Employees	_____	___ Earthquake
		___ Flood
		___ "All Risks"

___ Property in Transit .... Transit Risks
___ Fine Arts, Original Paintings .... "All Risks"
___ Valuable Records .... "All Risks"
___ Money & Securities .... "All Risks"
___ Plate Glass .... Accid. Break. & Vand.
___ Steam Boilers .... Explosion

LIABILITY	LIMITS OF LIABILITY
Public Liability	_____
___ Premises & Operations	
___ Contractual Liability	
___ Employees as Additional Insureds	
___ Personal Injury Endorsement	
___ Products Liability Endorsement	
___ Host Liquor Liability	_____
___ Liability for Damage to Leased Bldg.	_____
Auto Liability	_____
___ Owned Vehicles	
___ Physical Damage Endorsement	
___ Non-owned & "Hired Car" Coverage	
Umbrella Liability	_____
Directors', Officers', Trustees' Liability	_____

MISCELLANEOUS COVERAGES

___ Workers' Compensation
___ Treasurer's Qualifying Bond .... _____
___ Employee's Fidelity Bond .... _____
   New Construction
    ___ Certificates of Insurance from Contractor
    ___ Owner's Protective Liability
    ___ Builders' Risk Insurance

GLOSSARY

Actual cash value vs. Replacement cost. The basis of loss settlement under the standard fire insurance policy as well as most other property insurance policies is actual cash value. This is equivalent to market value for those types of personal property which are available in the used market (for example, automobiles, office machines, office furniture). For other types of property which are not generally available on the used market, actual cash value is recognized as replacement cost (new) less depreciation which is based on wear and tear and obsolescence. Usually the policy can be amended by endorsement to cover replacement cost (new) instead of actual cash value, provided the property is actually replaced. If property is not replaced, then loss settlement basis reverts to actual cash value.

Agreed amount clause/Amount of insurance clause. See Coinsurance.

All risks vs. Named peril. Most property insurance policies protect against loss by named peril such as fire, extended coverage, water damage, and the like, and are designated as "named peril" policies. In some cases a broader policy form designated as "all risks" is available; this form generally covers against all risks of physical loss or damage subject to certain designated exclusions.

Bailee/Bailor. When one person holds personal property belonging to another, the two persons are designated respectively as bailee and bailor. The bailor as owner has the "risk of loss" unless the parties have agreed otherwise, but the bailee will be responsible for loss or damage to the property if he is negligent, that is, fails to use a reasonable degree of care under the circumstances.

Blanket form. This is an insurance policy or policy form covering more than one type of property in a single amount or limit. For example, a blanket form covering library property may be written for a single amount of insurance and cover a number of buildings as well as the contents of those buildings including furniture and fixtures, equipment, books, library materials, and other tangible property.

Coinsurance. The coinsurance clause is an agreement or obligation of the library to carry insurance on its property to a specified percentage of the total value at the time of loss. Under the blanket form of policy 90 percent coinsurance is the most common. If the amount of insurance carried at the time of loss is less than the required percentage, the library will collect only a proportion of its loss. For example, if total value of property at the time of the loss is $100,000 and the coinsurance clause is 90 percent, the library should carry $90,000 insurance. If the library carries only $70,000 insurance, it will collect only 7/9 of each loss. When the policy contains a replacement cost endorsement, the coinsurance requirements apply to the replacement cost value rather than the actual cash value. (This concept of coinsurance is to be distinguished from its use in major medical expense policies where an 80 percent coinsurance clause means that the insured can recover only 80 percent of his or her loss.)

Fire insurance coverage also may be written with the "amount of insurance" clause (sometimes known also as the "agreed amount" clause). This clause is available upon filing a statement of current values (replacement cost or actual cash values, depending on the type of the policy) with the insurance company or the rating bureau. The amount of insurance is adjusted to 90 percent of the stated values and the insurance company attaches the "amount of insurance" clause. This waives the application of the coinsurance clause for the next 12 months.

Common law. This refers to the body of law, that is, the legal rules and principles which have grown out of case law. Where there are no state or federal statutes applying to a given legal proposition, then the courts will rely heavily on previous court decisions. The origin of the common law in the early years of our country was the English law.

Contractual liability. See Hold Harmless or Indemnity Agreements.

Designated exclusions. All insurance policies contain exclusions. These are fairly well standardized but may also, in some instances, be subject to modification. Modifications will depend upon the needs of the insured library and will require the consent of the insurance company.

Difference in (of) conditions (D.I.C. or D.O.C.). The term used in the insurance industry to designate a policy which provides broader coverage than the ordinary fire and extended coverage policy. It is essentially "all risk" with some limitations and exclusions and with a specific exclusion of loss or damage which is normally covered under the standard fire and extended coverage policy.

Floater policy. A policy designed to cover personal property which is likely to be moved from location to location. A floater policy commonly is used to insure such items as cameras and projection equipment, fine arts, and goods in transit, such as books in a bookmobile.

Hold harmless or Indemnity agreements. Agreements which provide that one party (usually a contractor or a lessee) will indemnify another (the owner or lessor) for liability for damage or injury as a result of certain acts, occurrences, or happenings. To the extent that these events are normally included under the liability insurance policy, they can be insured. For example, indemnification for bodily injury will be insurable; that for violation of a statute or municipal code will not. (The insurance coverage provided for hold harmless or indemnity agreements is generally known as contractual liability.)

Improvements and betterments. A legal term which applies to property installed by the tenant as part of a building which he leases. Legally, the property becomes a part of the building upon installation and the landlord has an insurable interest therein. However, the landlord may be under no obligation to repair or replace damage to improvements and betterments installed during the term of the lease. In such a case it is necessary that the tenant insure to cover his cost in repairing or replacing the improvements and betterments.

Liability for torts. A legal obligation may arise in two ways: (1) by contract or agreement, or (2) as a result of a tort. A tort is a private or civil (as distinguished from criminal) wrong committed by one person against another or against the property of another. The liability arises when the person who commits the wrong violates a duty to the injured person. Liability arising out of contract is considered to be a business risk and is generally not insurable. An exception is the hold harmless or indemnity agreement by which the insured contracts to indemnify another for his liability for accidents. Tort liability generally is insurable. The principal insurable tort is negligence, that is, the failure of the insured to use proper care in conducting his activities or business or in maintaining his property, as a result of which persons or property of others are injured. The so-called intentional torts, such as assault and battery and theft of property, are generally not insurable.

Package policy. A policy containing two or more coverages which can also be written separately.

Subrogation. A common-law principle by which one who indemnifies another for injury or damage is entitled to the indemnitee's rights against a third person who caused the injury. As applied to insurance, the insurance company who pays for collision damage to its insured's auto has the right of subrogation against the one who negligently caused the damage. More specifically for libraries, when an employee of a library who is a tenant in the building negligently causes fire damage to the building, the insurance company which pays the landlord for his damage may subrogate against the library. This creates a special problem for a library which is a tenant because its public liability insurance excludes coverage for liability for damage to property which it rents.

Tort. See Liability for torts.

Umbrella (Excess) Liability. This is excess liability insurance applying in addition to or above the limit of the basic (comprehensive public liability and auto liability) policies. It is usually broader than the basic policies. If a claim which is not covered by the basic policies should fall within the umbrella policy, a deductible or self-retention limit will apply, usually in the amount of $5,000 or $10,000.

Valued form. Contrary to the standard insurance practice of insuring to the extent of "actual cash value," some types of personal property may be insured on a valued form, that is, for a specified or agreed amount. Reimbursement in the event of loss is on the basis of this agreed amount rather than actual cash value at the time of the loss. This form of coverage generally applies to special types of property such as original paintings, fine arts, and the like, for which a market price or replacement cost is not easily established. It is also available under the Hartford Special Library form for books and library materials. When the term is used in connection with this policy and the valuable papers form, it indicates that the coinsurance clause does not apply. (Fire insurance rates are predicated on insurance to full value of the property—or to 80 or 90 percent of full value. For this reason a coinsurance clause is usually required, except on a valued form or policy where it is assumed that the value designated for the individual item of property is the full value.)

Z
683.5
M94

NOV 11 1977